Note for Librarians: A cataloguing record for this book is available from Library and Archives Canada at www.collectionscanada.ca/amicus/index-e.html
ISBN 1-4251-1220-x

Printed in Victoria, BC, Canada. Printed on paper with minimum 30% recycled fibre. Trafford's print shop runs on "green energy" from solar, wind and other environmentally-friendly power sources.

TRAFFORD
PUBLISHING™

Offices in Canada, USA, Ireland and UK

Book sales for North America and international:
Trafford Publishing, 6E–2333 Government St.,
Victoria, BC V8T 4P4 CANADA
phone 250 383 6864 (toll-free 1 888 232 4444)
fax 250 383 6804; email to orders@trafford.com
Book sales in Europe:
Trafford Publishing (UK) Limited, 9 Park End Street, 2nd Floor
Oxford, UK OX1 1HH UNITED KINGDOM
phone 44 (0)1865 722 113 (local rate 0845 230 9601)
facsimile 44 (0)1865 722 868; info.uk@trafford.com
Order online at:
trafford.com/06-2979

10 9 8 7 6 5 4 3 2

TABLE OF CONTENTS

CLEAR THE CLUTTER

STUFF

"Right from the time we are young we are given **STUFF**.
We learn to like **STUFF**.
As we grow up, we want even more **STUFF**.
We continually ask our parents for money so we
can buy **STUFF**.
Then, when we are of age, we get a job to buy **STUFF**.
We get a house into which we put our **STUFF**.
Needless to say, we must buy a car to haul our **STUFF**.
Because we soon get too much **STUFF**, our house
Becomes too small. So we get a bigger house.
Now we don't have enough **STUFF** for the big house.
So we buy more **STUFF**.
We need a new car because we have worn our
old car out carrying this **STUFF** around.
And on it goes. We never get around having all
the **STUFF** we want!"

Author Unknown

ACKNOWLEDGEMENT
SPECIAL ACKNOWLEDGEMENTS AND THANKS

I am so greatly indebted to the many wonderful contributors and participants who helped in the creation and expansion of this book in its original form.

Since 1994, "*Clear the Clutter & Simplify your Life*" has grown from one evening class, to nine locations, including one-day full workshops. The "*Clutter*" series are now offered as part of Lunch & Learn, Wellness Programs, as well as employee workshops / conferences and keynote talks.

In 1994 when I first "launched" the Clutter workshops, Ed Bailey and Linda Shaw helped and supported me to "spread-the-word" on the Clutter workshops and services. For this I thank them.

Thanks to my cousin, the late Nick Coles, for his great Clutter cartoons.

For six years I facilitated and offered Monthly Clutter Support Groups and thank all of those that attended for their active participation as well as their ideas and suggestions. We had much fun and great Clutter stories.

Thanks also to the following persons for teaching the "Clutter" classes in order to meet the demands made within the lower mainland. They are, Alison Roberts, Linda Shaw, Linda Chu, Elinor Warkentin, May Smith and Anne James.

Special thanks to Audrey Nawrocky, Coordinator of CES, Vancouver School Board for allowing me, twelve years ago to "launch" the Clutter workshops/classes, which still continue to grow.

Thanks to Janice Douglas, Director of Youth & Programs at the main Vancouver Public Library for allowing me to offer Clutter talks as part of the Healing Paths Series, four times a year, with 250 plus people attending — it is FUN and very enjoyable.

Thanks to Eddie and Rik at Pender Copy for all your help and support over the last 14 years — it has been a journey.

To my wonderful brothers and sisters and extended family, thank you for believing in me and helping me through those difficult times in my life, to my sister, Wendy in Vancouver, Canada for always being there for me, especially during my cancer journey, and to Michael New for just "being there", the late Glen Cropsey (you will always be missed and loved), and my good friends for their support, love and laughter. Dorothy Blandford, Sandra and David Craig, Marie Tomko, Vee Maurio, Len Comaniuk, Barb Davies and my wonderful friends in England, they are; John Styles, Peter, Terry, Mrs. "G" and David, Len, Paul, Brian and the late Jonathan Bratt. THANK YOU ALL for being my friend and being part of my life.

For V.P. you will always be special.

Special thanks to my Aunt Olive who is no longer with us but remains in our hearts for your wonderful stories and your shoe boxes filled with photographs and memories.

To my dear Dad who passed away so young, I miss you and thank you for your gifts, including your great sense of humour and kindness.

To the wonderful Staff and friends at St. Paul's Hospital, Vancouver, including the doctors and Dr. Perler for your help, support and care during my experience with cancer, during and after my recovery.

I dedicate this book to my Mum, who passed away suddenly at 78 years of age. Mum was a clutterbug and would have gotten a good laugh out of this project. We all miss you Mum.

Special thanks to the Universe for allowing me to share my skills, knowledge experiences and passion with you. I am truly thankful and grateful for all the wonderful people that have touched my life over the years, I am indeed blessed. Enjoy!

Special thanks to André Tassé for word processing, editing, proof-reading and supporting me in this project. Without his continuous help this book would not have happened. Thanks also to Sarah Campbell of Trafford Publishing for her on-going help and support.

"In character, in manner, in all things – the supreme excellence is simplicity".

– Longfellow

Talbot's Tips

- After eating, clean your dishes or put them in the dishwasher.

- If you have a recyclable item, put it in the recycle bin when you have done with it.

PREFACE

"Often people attempt to live their lives backwards: they try to have more things, or more money, in order to do more of what they want so that they will be happier. The way it actually works is the reverse: You must first be who you really are, then do what you need to do, in order to have what you want."

– Margaret Young

Life is not quite the same as it was. But then, it never really is. The pace of change does seem to be picking up. Like it or not, our lives are externally affected by technology, innovations, political decisions, the weather, and millions of daily events that take place in the world without our knowledge. Today, people seem to be busier than ever, running and trying to keep up with themselves and the Joneses.

We want it all and we want it now, but are we happy?

Looking back at my own life and growing up in a large family, being the eldest of seven children (3 boys and 4 girls), we never went without food on the table and a roof over our heads as well as clean, warm clothing. I remember when we had our first washing machine. Before then, whites were boiled (including handkerchiefs and all sheets and towels) in a large pot on the stove, washing hung out on lines to dry. On rainy or snowy days, we had lines hung from the ceiling in the room off the main kitchen, the scullery, as we call it in England. I remember when we were the first to have black and white television in our street. Suddenly, neighbours would "drop in." We had no clothes dryer for a long time, no microwave, no bread maker, no coffee maker or dishwasher (all dishes were washed and wiped by hand)...

Back then, like today, we still had seven days in a week and 24 hours in a day. How we used them was a choice, just as you have today.

When my Gran had her stroke, both she and Grandad moved in with us, and we went from nine persons to eleven – a full household, and we managed.

Being the eldest in the family, I was always the neat and tidy one, and I was also expected to help out. So, I "mastered" many of the survival skills at a young age. Of course, the other brothers and sisters were also expected to help out, some did and some managed to get away with doing very little. As the eldest, I did not have hand-me-downs, I was somewhat spoiled: this often happens in certain cultures.

When looking back at my childhood, it is clear to see how it has shaped me to be a well organised, clutter-free person.

Perhaps you've asked yourself the following questions: Were your parents clutterers / hoarderers? Have you inherited any of their traits? Are you rebelling? What clutter issue reminds you of your parents or even grand parents?

Where were you in the pecking order? If you grew up having hand-me-downs or clothing made by your Mum (and perhaps Mum was not the best seamstress), you might not have felt valued and now, as an adult, with your own earning power, you only buy the very best, whether or not you get yourself into debt. Or, you may have gone the other way: become very tight and frugal with spending on yourself as deep down, you do not feel worthy of nice things, yet you are kind and generous to other people.

If your family (like my Gran and Grandad) went through the depression and the war, you will over time receive messages like: "Money does not grow on trees," "Your dad had to work hard for that," "Be careful with that; it cost a lot of money," "You must think we are made of money." All of these messages, over time, will register with you and may affect your spending, collecting and how you live your life.

When most people think about clutter, they talk about physical clutter, looking at their household in their minds' eyes. However, sentimental, emotional and mental clutter can affect all other areas of your life. I have isolated six areas in particular. These are: <u>Household</u>, <u>Lifestyle</u>, <u>Career</u>, <u>Finances</u>, <u>Health</u> and <u>Relationships</u>.

Let me explain how these areas with clutter can have a domino effect in your life. Let us say that you have a problem at this time with your <u>finances</u>. This may affect your <u>health</u>, unable to sleep or sleep too much, eating too much or not enough, smoking or drinking. Your <u>relationships</u> may suffer, at home and at work. You are stressed, sometimes angry, you have outbursts, mood swings, to name a few. Your <u>career</u> may suffer: unable to concentrate, snappy to co-workers, feeling depressed... Your <u>lifestyle</u> will change dramatically. With much lesser income, unable to use your credit card or write cheques, you'll need to re-think all your buying habits... As you can see, "finances" that are "cluttered" and out of control have had an emotional and mental effect in four other areas of your life. We could go on: your <u>household</u> gets neglected as you come home too tired to even open the mail or answer the phone. You escape to the messy bedroom, hoping to avoid the situation.

If clutter in your "finances" is ruining your life, please refer to the "Finances" section in this book and seek credit counselling as soon as possible.

Change does not come easy for many of us, but we need to take baby steps in order to move forward. Sometimes, we need a real wake-up call! Have you ever watched the television program called "How Clean Is Your House?" What did you think? How did you react to some of the homes and people living in them? Perhaps you said to yourself: "My God! How can they live like that!?!" or something worse. However, it may just be a question of time before YOU are in that situation. Please remember that your clutter is often a symptom of something else – what are you trying to cover up?

All of us came in this world with NOTHING, we will all leave with

NOTHING, none of us will have a U-Haul behind our coffin with our china, clothing, computer, jewellery, etc.

When I think of "clutter," images of my dear Aunt Olive comes to mind. She was well known for not really loving housework, in fact, she would have NEVER been awarded the Good Housekeeping of the year. Aunt Olive loved to cook and entertain, often 15 or more people at a time, but the dishes often sat for days waiting to be washed. Vacuuming was not the highlight of the day, but her vacuum cleaner would sit in the main room, waiting to be plugged in and used. If you happened to visit, Aunt Olive would always say: "Oh, I was just going to vacuum, but I'll do it later. Move a few things off the sofa and find a space." Then, she would make a pot of tea and bring out a tray with something baked to eat. Of course, the coffee table was often covered in "stuff" as well as dust, and, as she was clearing it up, she would say: "I don't know where all this dust comes from, but never mind, a little dust did not kill anyone."

Aunt Olive loved her bingo, and on a Friday or Saturday night, if she won, she would order a take-out meal and we would go through her shoe boxes of old photos (Aunt Olive and my Dad were brother and sister) and tell her stories. The stories were always colourful, but, as I learned later, not always the truth. Often, four or five of us would bring over our photos and weave our own magical stories. Aunt Olive would set the theme: last vacation or best wedding you attended, and the laughter and joy would continue to three or four in the morning. From this experience, I learned a great deal about my Dad and his life and that one can lead a full life, and enjoy it even if one choses to live it in clutter and chaos.

Hopefully Clear the Clutter & Simplify Your Life will help you discover your own power to get organized, stay organized, and bring out your own personal and professional best. Throughout this book you will find points that are reiterated: the material comes from different sources through the years and I decided to leave the repetitions to reinforce points which I find are specially important.

This book is written with the intention to support thousands of people, and comes from many years of teaching the course to people from all backgrounds, nationalities and customs. What you might find redundant, someone else has never heard it before. Extract what you need and move on.

Finally, to live successfully, we must be willing to do four things:

1. Commit to being true to our inner integrity;

2. Shed our need to over control;

3. Act on what has heart and meaning, and;

4. Trust that there are no accidents

By clearing your clutter, having an on-going maintenance program you will have more time to do those things that bring you joy, pleasure and much happiness with those that you love.

Special blessing

Paul Talbot

October 2006

Vancouver, BC, Canada

WHO IS PAUL TALBOT?

He is an author, trainer, simplicity coach and certified Job Club Facilitator. His enthusiasm, laughter and passion for life is the key to his personality.

Paul Talbot started working with other people's clutter in 1994. At that time, he was a facilitator and counsellor for the Vancouver Friend's for Life Society, a non-profit group helping and supporting people living with life-threatening illnesses, their families and caregivers. He had a client that had moved several times and was about to move again, always with the same six or eight unopened boxes. It would appear that those boxes were never opened in four years plus. So Paul offered to sort out the boxes and help the client downsize and give away many items whilst he was still alive, all at the same time. In order to get organized, Paul felt the need to find some help and looking in a bookstore, he found, *Simplify Your Life*, by Elaine St. James. This book became Paul's model and from there his workshop was born. Also used was the book, *Don't Sweat the Small Stuff*, by Richard Carlson.

Since his personal experience with cancer in November 1998, he has again re-evaluated and simplified his life further. Paul believes if your stuff in your life, which includes relationships, no longer has value and purpose, it is time to let it or them go. Remember when you bring something new into your life, let something else go. It is not always necessary to fill the space or void. Live with the void for awhile.

Background / Experiences

Senior :lecturer / program Director at Central University of England, Birminham, England; Instructor at Vancouver Community College; Instructor for Continuing Education at Vancouver and New Westminster School Boards, Langara College and West End Community Centre. He also worked as a Private Secretary / Personal Assistant in London, England and Tripoli, Libya.

Paul owned and operated his own Personal / Employment Agency for nine years in Vancouver, BC and has worked for many non-profit agencies including The Vancouver Friends for Life Society (he was Program Director / Facilitator / Counsellor) and was co-founder of the HIV First Step Support / Program. As a certified Job Club Facilitator helping unemployed adults, Paul was facilitator / co-ordinator at Gordon Neighbourhood House and facilitator at the Immigrant Services Society and YMCA. He completed his HIV/AIDS Training at Aidsline, Birmingham, England and has volunteered in this area for many years offering support, counselling and facilitation of groups.

Accomplishment

He has written and published several books, newsletters and articles worldwide. He is the co-author of the North American book "TEELINE Shorthand" and one of the featured authors in "Positive Power People" published by Royal

Publishing, California, USA. He is creator / founder of the CLUTTER series which includes "Clear the Clutter and Simplify Your Life," "Clear the Clutter for Seniors," "Simple and Forgotten Things – Voluntary Simplicity" and "Be a Winner, Steps to Success." Paul has other books he is working on as well as audio presentations.

Paul has appeared on the CBC TV, Studio 4 and Plugged In for SHAW TV, BCTV, City Pulse TV as well as CBC Radio, Early Edition and CKNW with Rafe Mair. He has been featured in the Burnaby Newsleader, Family Circle, The Georgia Straight, The Globe & Mail, Shared Vision, Vancouver Courier and the Vancouver Sun.

He has been keynote speaker for many conferences and in-company presentations and continues to share his skills, knowledge and life-long experience with others. His unique style is his sense of humour, caring and support that he gives as well as his "gifted" way of communicating. He lives and loves life to the full and his passion is helping others reach and fulfill their dreams.

Mission Statement

To help individuals and organizations release their full potential by providing the means for training and developing opportunities.

Vision

A healthy world of well-balanced people who function by inspiring one another daily to greater heights and depths of love, joy, harmony and co-creativity.

Commitment

To offer an atmosphere of freedom and inspiration to support you sharing the gift of who you really are.

Vancouver School Board

School District No. 39 (Vancouver)

CONTINUING & INTERNATIONAL EDUCATION
1580 West Broadway
Vancouver, B.C.   V6J 5K8
Telephone: 604-713-4500
Fax: 604-713-4536

October 13, 2006

TO: Whom It May Concern

RE: Paul Talbot

It is my pleasure to write a recommendation for Paul Talbot.

Paul has been a valuable member of our Continuing Education teaching staff for over 20 years
and is a dedicated professional.   He has developed and delivered some of our most successful
courses over the years and continues to receive rave reviews from his students.

Paul's abilities are far ranging but in summary include:

➢ Workshop leader: Paul is able to successfully direct his program to suit the audience
whether in the corporate board room or in the night school classroom.

➢ Initiative: Paul always takes the initiative to pursue his interests with an eye to providing
learners with a new approach to acquiring knowledge.

➢ Self-motivation: Paul is a self-starter and has no difficulty working on his own.

➢ Organization: Paul is very organized and extremely accountable – as the "clutter guy" he
definitely "walks his talk".

➢ Reliability: Without a doubt you can rely on Paul to deliver what he promises in a timely
fashion; he completes and follows through on administrative detail and is a valued team
player.

If I can provide further information, please do not hesitate to contact me.

Sincerely,

Audrey Nawrocky
Program Coordinator

CONTINUING EDUCATION
New Westminster School District #40

835 Eighth Street, New Westminster, B.C., Canada   V3M 3S9
Telephone: (604) 517-6345   Fax: (604) 517-6302

October 4th 2006

To Whom It May Concern,

Reference: Paul Talbot

It is a pleasure for me to provide a reference regarding Paul Talbot. Paul has taught in our Night School Program since 1997. His expertise, efficiency and amiable personality have been an asset for students, staff and instructors alike. Paul's course evaluations indicate he is an exceptionally knowledgeable teacher who makes each class challenging and enjoyable. Students indicate that he is well prepared, articulate and provides a comprehensive coverage of the subject at hand. To quote from the course evaluations:

"Wonderful! Motivating! – a great instructor".
"Gave us the tools and ideas to work with" .
"Has given me food for thought and how to prioritize my life".
"Good practical examples – provided concrete tips to follow".

Paul brings to the Night School Program humor and enthusiasm to his field of study. As a Night School Programmer, I find it delightful to work with him and provide our adult learners an excellent opportunity to learn more about "Clear the Clutter", considering that his field of study has "taken off" country wide. He is a well known speaker and has remained loyal to our Night School Program.
For further information please don't hesitate to call 604-517-6345.

Sincerely,,

Karen Stubbs
Night School Programmer

Legal Services Society

Providing legal aid in British Columbia since 1979

Suite 400
510 Burrard Street
Vancouver, BC V6C 3A8

Tel: (604) 601-6000
Fax: (604) 682-0725
www.lss.bc.ca

Human Resources and Organizational Development

September 29, 2006

Paul Talbot
admin@dialaspeaker.com

P.O. Box 404
1195 Davie Street,
Vancouver, B.C.
Canada V6E 1N2

Dear Paul,

I'll admit when I signed up for "Clear the Clutter" I was expecting a rather dry and uninspiring hour. Instead I laughed a lot as I learned your easy-to-remember clutter clearing tips. Better yet, after leaving your "lunch and learn" session, I actually put some of those tips into motion and cleared up some clutter in my office before leaving work for the day.

I've had very positive comments from the others who attended your session. You (and your Aunt Olive) truly inspired us. We'll be asking you back soon and I will certainly recommend you to others.

Sincerely,

Christal Pendleton

Christal Pendleton
Human Resources Advisor

THE NON-PROFIT
DEBT SOLUTIONS
SERVICE

330 – 435 Columbia St.
New Westminster, BC V3L 5N8
TEL. 604.527.8999
FAX. 604.527.8008
TOLL FREE. 1.888.527.8999
www.nomoredebts.org

July 13, 2006

Paul Talbot
PO Box 404, 1195 Davie Street
Vancouver, BC   V6E 1N2

Dear Paul,

Re: Lunch and Learn Presentation – June 23, 2006

Paul, thank you so much for your entertaining and enlightening presentation to the staff at the Credit Counselling Society!

Though the time for the presentation was brief (over lunch), it encouraged us to closely examine ourselves and motivated us to take on the challenge of "clearing the clutter" in all facets of our life. Your presentation helped us think about why we allow clutter in our life and provided us with real solutions on how to get rid of the clutter.

On behalf of our entire organization, thank you, again, Paul!

Wishing you continued success,

CREDIT COUNSELLING SOCIETY

Monica Loeppky
Program Manager

City of Richmond

6911 No. 3 Road, Richmond, BC V6Y 2C1
Telephone (604) 276-4000
www.city.richmond.bc.ca

Rick Thomas, EdD
Manager, People & Organization Development
City of Richmond
6911 No. 3 Road
Richmond, B.C. V6Y 2C1

March 2005

Paul Talbot
PO Box 404
1195 Davie Street
Vancouver, B.C. V6E 1N2

Dear Paul,

Thank you, Paul, for jump-starting 2005 with your "Clear the Clutter and Simplify Your Life" workshop. As you know, the workshop was attended by over eighty employees of the City of Richmond, with rave reviews.

Evaluations of your sessions indicated that you provided some well-needed tips and techniques that people can immediately put into place which will allow them to achieve a more simplified, and clutter free, life – both at work and home. The activities were well received and you were given top marks for participant engagement. The only criticism was that you left everyone wanting more, which is certainly a positive testament to your skill as a presenter and the timely and relevant content matter.

Thanks again, Paul!

Regards,

Richard B. (Rick) Thomas, EdD

RCU
City of Richmond's Corporate U

RICHMOND
Island City, by Nature

1447639

350 West Georgia St.
Vancouver, B.C.
Canada V6B 6B1

Vancouver Public Library

Office of The Youth Services
& Programming Director

February 6, 2004

To whom it may concern

On behalf of the Vancouver Public Library, I am happy to write a letter of recommendation for Paul Talbot as a speaker. Paul has done eight events with us since September 2002. Each time he has had a significant audience and garnered an enthusiastic response. The most recent event had a turnout of approximately 300 people!

As co-founder of the End the Clutter International organization, Paul also works with the library to host community events, educating the public on the concepts of "reduce, reuse, recycle." His wit and humour turn the most odious of chores, "clearing clutter" into a positive and rewarding exercise. People love to stay after to talk with him and many end up going to his free support groups. While he offers many tips on simplifying our lives, many of the audience also return time and again to be encouraged with entertainment and laughter.

I would highly recommend Paul Talbot as a speaker for many groups and a variety of occasions.

Yours most sincerely,

Janice Douglas,
Youth Services & Programming Director,
Vancouver Public Library
(604) 331-4035
janicdou@vpl.vancouver.bc.ca

JD:ah

H:\CORRESP\PaulTalbot2004recommendationletter.doc

Funded by the
City of Vancouver

Printed on Recycled Paper

HOW TO USE THE SECTION MARKED 'NOTES'

Many of you will have your own experience of clearing clutter. Use the *'Notes'* section and write them down or use them as reminders.

You may find that ideas come to mind, or you see and read an article you want to share. Write this information down in the *'Notes'* column.

Talbot's Tips

- Get a fresh start. Clean out your closet, be ruthless, if you have NOT worn it in the last year or so, or it does not fit, let it go! Someone else out there, I am sure, would appreciate it.

- Items that you LOVE but need mended or altered, do it NOW, otherwise, let them go.

- Stop trying to dress like the fashion pages. Learn to wear what suits you, be smart, professional with that pulled-together look. Dress for your career and age appropriate. If necessary, hire an Image Consultant.

IDENTIFY THE CLUTTER PROBLEMS:
Suggested guidelines for results.

In this section, you will find entertaining and revealing ways to discover if clutter is actually an issue in your life (or the life of people around you). Interesting quizzes, point forms and quotes will get you started in thinking about your life and hopefully move you forward.

The clutter issues raised may be emotional and sentimental and therefore uncomfortable for you at times. It is normal for a person to feel overwhelmed by these issues. Most of us do not accept change very well in our lives. This is simply the time to take a break, to put the book down, to re-evaluate and give yourself some space before moving on.

ARE YOU A CLUTTERBUG?

Grab a pencil (if you can find one) and take the following quiz.

1 Do you hang onto clothes that don't fit or are out of date?
    YES ☐   No ☐

2 Do you keep stacks of old newspapers and magazines?
    YES ☐   No ☐

3 Has your electricity or telephone EVER been turned off simply because you lost the bill?
    YES ☐   No ☐

4 Do you own appliances or gadgets that you NEVER use?
    YES ☐   No ☐

5 Do you have tons of your kids' school papers (or yours) from kindergarten through college?
    YES ☐   No ☐

6 Do you have hundreds of photographs that you keep meaning to put in albums?
    YES ☐   No ☐

7 Do you have more than ONE junk drawer for gewgaws, dohickey and parts to unidentified appliances?
    YES ☐   No ☐

8 Are you storing heirlooms — furniture, china — that you haven't used for years?
    YES ☐   No ☐

9 Do you have things that have been waiting for months to be repaired or cleaned?
    YES ☐   No ☐

10 Is the clutter in your life so unmanageable that you don't know where to begin?
    YES ☐   No ☐

TOTALS: YES's _____   No's _____

SCORING:
Give yourself one point for each "YES" answer.

1-2 Good, you are not overwhelmed with clutter, but chances are you've got a few hot spots.

3-5 Uh-oh. Clutter is probably starting to put a permanent crease in your brow.

6-plus RED ALERT. You've got clutter crisis on your hands. Take control or get help.

CLUTTERBUSTERS TO LIVE BY

Here is a three-step process.

1. Figure it out. Develop an overall strategy and define your priorities. Stop making excuses, stop procrastinating, think about how much time and money it takes to keep clutter.

2. Dig out. Getting rid of things will be easier if you turn off the phone (let the machine get it), don't accept interruptions or distractions.

3. Keep it out. Remember the 'In-and-Out' rule. Something new in, something old OUT. Have a place for everything and everything in its place.

Remember: **Do it, read it, pay it, file it and throw the rest out.**

"Life is about community, hobbies and friends. Take time to enjoy them."

- Howard Richardson, Vice-President
Right Management Consultants, Toronto

How Do I Know If I Am a Clutterer???

Ask yourself the following questions and, if you answer "Yes" to three or more, there is a chance you are a clutterer or on your way to becoming one.

- Have you tried to clean up from time to time but unable to stick to it?

- Do you have more possessions or 'stuff' in your life than you can handle?

- Do you rent storage space to house items you never use?

- Do you collect things to give to others?

- Are you embarrassed to have people over because your home is never presentable?

- Do you feel you are living in clutter, chaos and confusion?

- Do you spend time looking for things that are hard to find because of clutter?

- Does the problem seem to be growing?

- Do you find it difficult to dispose of many things, oven those you have not used in years?

- Do you use distractions to escape from your clutter?

- Do you miss deadlines or abandon projects because you cannot find the paperwork or materials you need to finish the work?

- Is your clutter causing problems in your relationships?

- Are you easily sidetracked, moving from one project to another without finishing any of them?

- Do you hesitate sharing about this clutter problem because you are ashamed?

- Do you believe there is all the time in the world to clean your house, finish those projects and read all those piles of old magazines?

The Oxford English Dictionary defines "Clutter" as ... "a crowded and untidy collection of things..." In Feng Shui, the centuries old Chinese method of achieving physical and spiritual harmony, they talk about "clutter" as "stuck energy."

"Clutter" or "Stuck Energy" can be physical, mental (invisible), emotional and/or sentimental. This causes your life to be out of balance. "Clear the Clutter and Simplify your Life" workshop looks at:

- Household
- Lifestyles
- Finances
- Job / Career
- Health
- Relationships
- Core Simplicity

SYMPTOMS OF WORKING & LIVING WITH CLUTTER

- Stress
- Confusion
- Frustration
- Overwhelmed
- Procrastination
- Unproductive
- Tired, low energy
- Numbness, avoiding tasks or situations
- Lack of focus
- A sense of panic when you need to find something
- Feeling stuck
- Spinning your wheels
- Dissatisfied with yourself

THE SIX COSTS OF CLUTTER

Cost #1 – Hard-Earned Money
How many times have you come home from the store with more than you intended to buy?

Cost #2 – Cleaning Time
Once you bring something into your home, you will have to maintain it by dusting and cleaning. You are paying with your time.

Cost #3 – Happiness
If you do not like the dress, knickknacks, bookshelf, etc. any more, get rid of it. If it does not make you happy, get rid of it. Trust me, you will feel lighter and liberated once you do.

Cost #4 – Higher House Payments
All those extra things are taking up valuable space in your home. Or worse, perhaps you are renting storage space just so you can hang onto items you will never use. Get rid of excess stuff. It is costing you money.

Cost #5 – Time and Frustration

How much time do you spend looking for everyday items? What about items that you know you have but just cannot find? What items do you use on a regular basis and which ones can go?

Cost #6 – Self-Esteem

Did you break into a cold sweat the last time somebody dropped by unexpectedly? Being ashamed of your home and clutter is no way to live. Clear out the clutter and welcome your friends back into your life.

Make the change today. Throw it away. Give it away. Donate it or turn it into cash.

TEN TIPS FOR CLEARING YOUR CLUTTER

1. Surround yourself only with things you love or that serve a regular, useful function.
2. Deal with things on a daily basis – recycle papers and magazines.
3. If you must hold onto articles of interest, file them in a designated place. Don't keep piles of useless paper.
4. Never go to bed with a sink full of dirty dishes. Not a pretty sight first thing in the morning.
5. Pick things up off the floor. We invest a lot of money in our clothes and putting them away means less washing and dry cleaning and they last longer.
6. Divide and conquer. Put like items with like and give everything in your house a home.
7. Don't keep all your children's drawings, just the ones that really mean something to you. Even Picasso did the odd dodgy sketch. Your little masters won't thank you for keeping them when they are famous.
8. Ladies, purge your beauty products.
9. Why keep photographs that make you look bad? Bin them.
10. Revisit sentimental objects, letters, cards. Ask yourself if you really want to keep them.

GOOD LUCK!

26 MORE ANTI-CLUTTER TIPS

Finding time

1. Get up half an hour earlier and do one small job.
2. Get a portable phone; you can do two things at once.
3. Learn to program your VCR. Watch the show later, after your chores are done.
4. Distracted by TV? Set a card table and chair. Sort papers, polish shoes, fold laundry, put photos in albums. Much more motivating than a couch.

Systems

5. Bought new piece of clothing? Toss an old one.
6. Turn your daily planner into a vertical file. Tuck bills, ticket and invites into the date you need to pay or use them.
7. Loading the dishwasher, put all spoons in one section of utensil basket; same with forks, etc. Saves sorting after.
8. Shoes in boxes? Glue Polaroids on the end.
9. Never go up or downstairs empty handed. Leave box or basket at top and bottom, fill with items going up or down: make one trip a day.
10. Put what you use most often where it's easier to reach. This seems obvious, but check your drawers and kitchen cupboards.
11. Can't bear to toss it? Put it all in a box, seal, date but DON'T label it. If you haven't opened it after one year, toss it without opening!

Tossing stuff

12. Giving your stuff to charity takes the sting out of parting.
13. Old towels and blankets not suitable (but clean) for charities can go to animal shelters.
14. 'Uncollect' your collection of frogs, match books, whatever – and tell gift givers!

Storage

15. Store things logically: like stuff with like stuff. Label every storage box.
16. Buy matching set of clear food storage containers. Square ones take up less room.
17. Best storage: clear containers with lids.
18. Use what you have; old pillow cases for storing sheets, stuffed animals; any decorative basket is instant storage for something.
19. Deep closets? Stick mirror squares on ceiling to see what's at the back.
20. Replace solid drawer fronts with plexi.
21. Buy functional furniture that has storage space.

Finding stuff later

22. Make a list or index detailing where you have put items e.g. red box under bed contains costume party items.

Paper chase

23. To remove your name from junk mail mailing lists, contact your local post office for details. "No Junk Mail" 3"x3" sticker or label inside or near your mailbox.
24. Immediately get rid of circulars enclosed in bills.
25. Keep bank records for six years; income tax returns for seven; home improvement records until you sell the house.

Tip: More ideas?

26. _Clutter Control_ by Jeff Campbell (Dell Trade Paperback). The ultimate how-to book, available in libraries.

Talbot's Tips

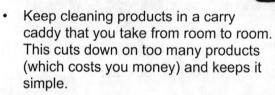

- One of the greatest ways to
  help children in school
  is to have them teach YOU
  what they are learning.

- Keep cleaning products in a carry
  caddy that you take from room to room.
  This cuts down on too many products
  (which costs you money) and keeps it
  simple.

TEN BASIC LAWS

In the late 70's and 80's we all bought into bigger is better, and more is even better. How many TV's, VCR's, dinner sets, cars and clothes did you have?

Was, or is, your life run by your daily planner, to-do lists, phone logs? How much time are you spending with your family and friends? Do you have fun in your life, or is it just one long merry-go-round? What does your life feel like? Stop and truly take a long look at where you are and what is going on with you and those you love.

Remember, keep value and purpose in your life.

Here are the Ten Basic Laws of Stuff taken from the book *The Complete Idiot's Guide to Organizing Your Life*, by Georgene Lockwood, published by Alpha Books:

1. Stuff breeds.

2. Useless stuff crowds out the good stuff.

3. Dust loves stuff.

4. Stuff loves to stay where it lands.

5. Stuff expands to fill space available.

6. Over time, stuff becomes invisible.

7. Stuff costs you money more than once.

8. Stuff has a powerful effect on your state of mind.

9. Stuff takes on value: only when it is used.

10. Stuff doesn't make you happy, you do!

As you go through this list, you may want to give examples and expand on it.

Example:

- If you start by leaving mail and papers on the table, usually by the end of the week, the table is covered with stuff.

- If you put something down, it will stay there until you, or someone else, moves it.

- If you have a four-drawer filing cabinet, you will find a way of filling it – swap it for a two-drawer!

Albert Einstein's Three Rules of Work:

1 Out of clutter, find simplicity.

2 From discord, find harmony.

3 In the middle of difficulty lies opportunity.

Here are some ideas and thoughts from the book, *Organizing from the Inside Out*, by Julie Morgenstern:

Fact: Organizing is a skill

Before you start working on your clutter, ask yourself five basic questions:

1. What's working?

2. What's not working?

3. What items are the most essential to you in terms of value and purpose?

4. Why do you want to get organized?

5. What's causing the problems?

Now, look at the total picture. Look at obstacles or stuff that are holding you back from being organized. Organize before buying storage units. Where will you put them? Will they fit?

Here are three easy rules to review before starting to clear your clutter.

1. **Analyse:** Step back to take stock of your current situation. Where you are, where you

are going, what's holding you back, and why it's important for you to get there.

2. **Strategize:** Create a plan of action for the physical transformations of your space, including a realistic time schedule for making it happen.

3. **Attack:** Methodically dive into the clutter, sorting and arranging items to reflect the way you think, making sure you see visible, dramatic results as you work.

Remember the 80:20% rule: We only use about 20% of what we own, the other 80% is stuff we once used, feel we should use, or think we might use some day.

Clutter occurs on three levels:

1. Technical Error — need fixing.

2. External Realities — beyond your control.

3. Psychological Obstacles — only you can pinpoint what's holding you hack.

Here are some clutter issues that we have or have had.

- Items have no home.

- More stuff than storage space.

- Out of sight, out of mind.

- Organizing is boring.

- Lack of time.

- Spouse or roommate is a clutterbug.

- Apartment, flat or house is too small, no storage space.

- Suffering from constant interruptions.

- Pressure to respond to letters, faxes, newspapers, and magazines.

- Getting rid of anything is a disturbing prospect.

- Constant need to buy more stuff.

- Tendencies to display everything collected.

- More time is spend organizing and reorganizing than working or having fun.

- The cluttered state of our home keep us from letting people visit us.

- Accumulated clutter goes back 10 to 15 years or more: it's overwhelming.

- Need for abundance. Fear or scarcity.

- Fear of success or failure.

- Unclear goals and priorities.

- Sentimental attachment.

- Need for perfection.

- Need for distraction.

For Dramatic Results

- Attack the visible first.

- Quick sort for quick results.

- Avoid zigzag organizing.

From the book, *From the Inside Out*, Julie Morgenstern uses her SPACE formula:

S =   sort, group similar items together.

P =   purge, decide what to let go and keep.

A =   assign a home to each item.

C =   containerize, containers make it easy for locating and labelling.

E =   equalize, keep the system going, keep it simple, establish a regular routine for staying on track.

Talbot's Tips

- Be ruthless and clean out all
  your old cosmetics –
  they too have a shelf life.

- Group similar things together in
  bins or baskets.

- Paint a finishing tackle box for holding
  your cosmetics or jewellery – they have
  lots of storage and compartments.

THE PROCESS

This is when you need to make an appointment and commitment to yourself that you will start the de-cluttering process. Human nature being what it is, we often bite off more than we can chew. Therefore, this section will help you break down your task in small, manageable and achievable steps.

Hopefully, you will be able to easily identify the pages that talks about the specific area that needs your immediate attention. From general guidelines to specifics, this section will take you step by step through each room of your house, through your workplace, lifestyle, finances, health issues, relationships and more...

Try to do a minimum of two hours per week on the clearing and sorting of your clutter.

Start by setting goals for yourself. What is a goal? A goal is something that you want to do, to be, or to have, like clearing the clutter in the bedroom.

CLUTTER ACTION PLAN

Week of: From: _____ to _____

Clutter can be physical, sentimental, emotional or mental. Its areas are:
Household, Lifestyle, Career, Finances, Health, Relationships

AREAS I WISH TO WORK ON THIS WEEK:

_____
_____
_____
_____
_____
_____
_____

RESULTS I WISH TO ACHIEVE:

_____
_____
_____

SUCCESSES THIS WEEK INCLUDE:

_____
_____
_____

WHY SET GOALS?

Why Set Goals?

- They give you life direction.
- They give you control over your life.
- They give you something to work for.
- They give you a feeling of accomplishment.
- They help you to feel responsible for your actions.

Keys to Setting Successful Goals

These are some questions to ask yourself when you're planning your next goal:

- Evaluate your problem(s).
- Your main goal must be something that you really want.
- You must believe that it is possible for you to reach your goal: is it achievable?
- Be specific and realistic:
- Set a specific plan by identifying stepping stones.
- Break down your major goal in smaller steps
- Identify any obstacles. Plan ways to overcome those obstacles.
- Set some time lines.
- Be ready and willing to ask for help.

Ask Yourself...

- Do I keep things just in case?
- What do I do with unwanted gifts?

- Do I keep up with my letter writing?

- Am I comfortable with the newspapers and magazines around the house?

- Can I easily find names, addresses and phone numbers when I need them?

- Do I have clutter in the car and at the office?

- My clutter includes: books, papers, photos, magazines, cards and collections of spoons, teddy bears and bone china... help!

- Why am I holding on to other people's clutter?

- So-called friends that only call me when they want something ... what's in it for me?

- Am I taking care of me, or am I holding onto clutter?

Remember that you may have to go through your clutter several times before you can finally let go. When you let the clutter go, there will be a void. What will you fill it with?

How to Keep Yourself Motivated

- Post your goals.

- Use before and after photos.

- Reward yourself along the way.

- Make it fun.

- Work with a buddy.

Define your zones and areas

Example: **Bill Paying**

Activities	Supplies	Storage Units
Bill Paying	Bills to Pay	Desk or
	Credit Cards	Drawer
	Bank Statements	
	Envelops, labels,	
	stamps,	
	calculator, pen,	
	stapler or	
	direct phone	
	information	

Create a simple filing system for all of your paperwork, paid bills and receipts.

Clear the clutter and simplify your life.

- If you take it out, put it back.

- If you open it, close it.

- If you throw it down, pick it up.

- If you take it off, hang it up.

Talbot's Tips

- When you are ready to de-clutter, ... PLAN. Start small, a drawer, bathroom or something manageable. Complete the task and at the end, reward yourself.

- Set the timer for each task you are working on. This will help keep you on track and focussed.

YOUR HOUSEHOLD

Let's start by reducing the clutter in your home. Can you downsize? Do you want to?

Items you need before you start:
- Empty boxes: not the ones that you have that are already filled up with stuff.
- Garbage bags
- Markers and pens
- A timer: The timer is used to see how much you achieve in 30 to 60 minutes. Remember some of us get bored very easily.
- Appointment book: Make an appointment with yourself. Write it down as you would for a doctor or dentist. Make a commitment.
- Labels. You may want to mark ahead using comments such as:
  - *Bathroom* or other rooms. Items that belong elsewhere.
  - *Sister*
  - *Friend*s: name those friends you want to give to.
  - *Charities:* name those charities you want to give to.
  - *Co-worker:* name those that might be interested in your stuff.
  - *Maybes* are items that maybe you'll keep or not (date that label and revisit in 3-6 months)?
  - *Recycle Bins*

If your clutter is overwhelming, you may want to start with something small, like the bathroom or a junk drawer, or...

CLEAR THE CLUTTER©

ACTION PLAN

Date Started: _____

Date Finished: _____

Step 1: Create an inventory of all the clutter you wish to get rid of.

Step 2: Quickly try to place items in appropriate category.

ITEM	TRASH	RECYCLE	GIVE AWAY (friends/family)	DONATE (charity)	STORAGE	SELL
CLOTHING & ACCESSORIES						
FURNITURE						
HOUSEWARES						
ANTIQUES & COLLECTIBLES						
CDs, TAPES, RECORDS & BOOKS						
TOYS						
ELECTRONICS						
TOOLS & EQUIPMENT						
APPLIANCES						
COMPUTER & RELATED ITEMS						
LINEN						
OTHER						

Step 3: Look at what you have placed in the sell column

- Make sure you want to sell it
- Make sure it is sellable
- Make sure you have the time and energy to sell it
- Make any necessary changes to that list

CLEAR THE CLUTTER©   **ACTION PLAN** (continued)

Step 4: Lets look at where you can sell your clutter.

Item	Classified ads	Garage sales	Flea markets	Auctions	Consignment stores	Antique stores	Antique dealers	Vintage stores
CLOTHING & ACCESSORIES								
FURNITURE								
HOUSEWARES								
ANTIQUES & COLLECTIBLES								
CDs, TAPES, RECORDS & BOOKS								
TOYS								
ELECTRONICS								
TOOLS & EQUIPMENT								
APPLIANCES								
COMPUTER & RELATED ITEMS								
LINEN								
OTHER								

Step 5: Start making all the calls and start turning your clutter into cash!

Step 6: Still feeling overwhelmed? Maybe time to revisit the lis or consider bringing in a professional or get some support to move through the process.

Resource: Jo-Arne Lauzer – www.secondhandsavvy.com

Need help? Contact Paul Talbot,

No Clutter Guy, at

www.noclutterguy.com

Suggested Ways to Store Household Information
Several options include:

Sort by category –	financial, vital records, travels
Sort by person –	bank accounts, medical records, income tax
Sort in Alpha order –	addresses, bank information, car papers

Suggestions for household filing include:

Financial
- banking statements
- bills to pay
- budget
- credit cards
- financial statements
- income tax – the current year
- insurance (home, life, car, mortgage)
- investment records
- loan records
- pay stubs
- pension plan records
- property
- receipts (appliances, arts and antiques, clothing, furniture, home appliance, home repairs, taxes)

Vital records
- car records
- certificates (adoption, birth, death, citizenship, marriage, divorce, name change)
- education records or transcripts
- employment information
- household inventory
- income tax – previous years
- legal records
- medical records
- power of attorney
- résumé
- vital documents and map of location
- wills

Lifestyle
- address lists
- airmiles
- charitable organizations
- church information
- classes
- correspondence
- entertainment
- events
- fitness
- health
- humour
- memorabilia
- past calendars
- pets
- recipes
- restaurants
- travel
- weekends

Handling Paper

Many published books will have several suggestions. Here is a simple, but effective way of handling household incoming mail.

Consider purchasing two plastic baskets to be used as in-baskets. As you gather the mail from the mailbox or mat and if you are short of time, do a quick sort. In basket one, place all letters, bills and coupons, especially if they have an expiry date on them. In basket two, place all newspapers, flyers, subscriptions and other stuff in this basket.

By using these in-baskets, it will keep all mail together, in one place as well as being portable. When you have time, take basket one and go through each item carefully, making a decision for each one. You can also add file folders with pockets to place all the bills that have to be paid. Always circle the date due. You can always pay bills by direct debit. As you go through basket one, make a decision. Letters to be answered or information needed, have a separate file folder. there are several kinds on the market. Find the one that best suits your needs.

Coupons; check the expiry date. If you don't think you will use them, pass them on to family members, friends or co-workers. If you live in an apartment building, place them on a general notice board.

If you have no time to read them, place articles, magazines and newspapers in basket two. As this is portable, take the time out one evening and go through. Always check the date and the year, place older items in the recycling bin, if they are too old. If you think you may need this article at a later date, create a simple log for recording the same.

Your log should be in a three ring binder with tabs either under _Topics_ or _A-Z_. Remember to file it where you know you can find it. Ask yourself, "Do I file this before or after the tab?" Be consistent. File using plastic protectors.

Magazines or articles – do you need to keep the whole thing, or can you just photocopy what you need? Pass the complete magazine or paper on to others in its complete form. Make friends with your library.

Your in-coming mail will determine the kind of system you need. Keep your in-baskets in one place. This keeps clutter away from tabletops, counters and other flat surfaces. If you cannot go through your mail daily, make an appointment with yourself to do it once a week.

Consider the five-folder system (or five-box method):

1. for Act On – number one priority.

2. for Pass On.

3. for File.

4. for Reading.

5. for Discard or Recycle.

Sorting Piles of Paper

First Step: Sort. Have empty boxes or trays with labels on. Suggested headings can include:

- Articles.
- Magazines.
- Give or Mail To?
- Recycle.
- File.
- Purchase Receipts.
- Business Cards.
- Maybe.

Next step: Once sorted, go through each box or tray and make a decision. Handle each piece of paper only once. If uncertain of what to do, place in the Maybe box, maybe I'll keep, or maybe I'll let go. When in doubt, let it go (unless it is income tax related: by law, you are bound to keep it for seven years).

When looking at articles, news clipping and magazines, first look at the year and the date. Is it too old and out of date? If so, let it go.

Enter the basic details including name, topic, subject, year and date into your master log. Otherwise you can place it in the recycle bin.

Complete one pile at a time. Consider breaking the larger piles into smaller ones. Reward yourself as you work through the paper piles.

A must: Allocate time each week to work on your papers. Write it down. In other words, make an appointment with yourself.

Filing cabinets or storage units? Before you can file, you may have to go through your units that are breaking at the seam with stuffed papers. Weed out the papers, be ruthless. Ask yourself as you go through each file, "When was the last time I looked at this? Do I need it? What would be the worst thing that could happen to me if I dumped it?" Be honest with yourself.

Make friends with your library. Use your computer more for research and information gathering if necessary.

Bathroom

A small room for most of us, but one that needs to be cleaned out on a regular basis.

You can tell a great deal about a person by the state of their bathroom.

- Out dated medicines and lotions. Place in a bag and take to your local pharmacist or chemist. Be very careful what you do with half empty bottles of pills. Again, bag them with your medicines.

- Free samples of shampoo, conditioners and soaps. If you have no intention of using them, donate it to local charities, senior citizens homes. Someone I know puts them in small Christmas bags and leaves the bags by each door in the apartment building she lives in. Recycle and share.

- Toilet rolls. You do not need one gross in the cupboards. Leave three or four spare and put the others elsewhere.

- Spare towels. These can be rolled and placed in wicker baskets or in a wine rack. You only need two or three in the bathroom, depending on the number of people living in the household.

- Hand towels. Pretty, but often people are afraid to use them. Same with guest soap. Looks too pretty, so people don't use them. They sit there and gather dust.

- Under the sink racks. Use these for storing things.

- Cosmetics. Check your cosmetics. Throw out items that are outdated or not your colour. Be ruthless. Remember, fashions change and so do you.

- Duplicate items. Pack in a toilet bag for your next weekend away. Be prepared!

Bedroom

Many of us have too many clothes. Some too small, others too large, wrong colour or style. Chances are, if you have not worn them within the last twelve months, you never will.

First, pick a day and time when you can do this without interruptions. You need to do this activity first on your own.

Make sure that the bed is clear (hopefully you have no clutter there) and start laying items from your closet on the bed. Do this in sections.

You may want to break the items down into seasons such as Spring, Summer, Winter and Fall, as well as into casual, office, dressy or evening.

Now comes the difficult part. You need to try on each piece of clothing and be honest with yourself. Perhaps you have changed your hair colour and image. Do your clothes reflect that? If you are uncertain, you have two options:

1.   Have a friend over that will be honest on giving you feedback; or

2.   Hire an Image Consultant, most Yellow Pages will have listing for these professionals.

As you go through your wardrobe, get rid of all the wire hangers. Wire hangers ruin your clothes. Instead of wire, invest in wooden hangers for suits and sturdy plastic ones for shirts and blouses. One colour hanger in the closet looks better organized, otherwise you can colour code.

Under the section named *'Handouts'* in the workbook / manual, use the Closet Inventory Sheet supplied.

Consignment Stores and Shops

Many consignment stores will split on a 50/50 basis. Hold items are usually held for up to three months. During that time, the stores may reduce the suggested selling price to move inventory. Check the Yellow Pages for consignment stores or ask friends if they can recommend some.

If you want, you can advertise in your local newspapers or put free advertisements in your local community centres. Laundromats, colleges and universities are often places that have space set aside for free advertising on boards.

My suggestion:

I like to give some of my stuff away to charities and similar organizations. Other stuff is allocated to consignment stores, this method often can reduce and take away the guilt of buying. In turn, I hopefully get some of the investment back.

Another note:

Some consignment scores will only take designer labels and most have a set time of day to receive your items. It is best to telephone ahead to ensure that the right person will be there to take your items in, price them and complete the paperwork.

If you are uncertain about your clothing, place those items in a maybe box, label the box and date it. If you have an instant camera, take photographs of the items and attach it to the front of the box. Store the box for six to twelve months. In that time, if you have not touched anything in the box and none of the items were missed, then pass the whole box on to a charity. Make a decision!

If you have had the same look for the past ten years, it may be time for a change. You may have to go through your closet two or three times before you are truly ready to start to pare down. Be honest and ruthless with yourself. Most of us have too much of everything and we often only wear the few favourites that we have.

This includes:

- Shoes. Do they fit? Do they need to be repaired? What will you wear with them? Again, be honest with yourself.

- Bags and purses. This can also date your look. Cheek inside each item to see that there are no lost pens, notes, or even money.

- Ties, for men. Again, these items can date your look.

- Socks. Throw out the ones with holes in and those that are mismatched.

- Underwear. Treat yourself like a first class person each day. Wear sexy ones if they make you feel good. As Mum always said "You never know if you will get in an accident today", so wear clean underwear. Those with holes or broken elastics can be used as cleaning rags. Read the section titled *"Underwear"* in the book called *True Love,* by Robert Fulghum, pages 204 to 208. The section is quite a wonderful and uplifting story.

- Jewellery. Sort out costume pieces from the real items. Do you wear it? How often? Coffee mug racks are great for necklaces and bracelets. Fishing tackle boxes are great for using since they have lots of compartments. Ice cube trays can also double for storing your earrings.

After cleaning out the closets in your bedroom, go through each drawer, under the bed or other places that you store and keep stuff.

Now, take a long look at the total room. Why do you want to get organized? Do you want ...

- a peaceful retreat.

- a better night sleep.

- a sense of control.

- to get more reading and writing done.

Plan your zones. You may need to rearrange the furniture, get rid of some or swap pieces with someone else.

Zones or areas

Activities	**Supplies**	**Storage Units**
Reading	Magazines	Bedside table
	Books	
	Reading	
	Glasses	
	Good Lamp	

If you have more than one bedroom, you may want to repeat this exercise, or have others in the household start the clutter project. If other household members join in, make sure that they understand all of the benefits such as turning items into cash, getting organized and letting go of stress because they can never find anything.

Make it fun!

Closet Inventory

Instructions:

- Remove all garments from your closet that have not been worn in the past year.

- Separate your fall and spring clothing into opposite ends of the closet or into separate closets, if possible.

- Arrange your clothes by type such as dresses, suits, pants or skirts – all within a season.

- List your wardrobe 'haves' and 'needs' below and bring your closet inventory to the store with you when you begin to rebuild your wardrobe. Don't forget to bring that favourite item as well. You might want to build an outfit or wardrobe around it.

CLOSET INVENTORY

Clothing	Have	Need	Colour	Description	Works well with ....
Suits					
Jackets					
Blouses					
Sweaters					
Skirts					

CLOSET INVENTORY

Clothing	Have	Need	Colour	Description	Works well with ....
Pants					
Shirts					
Shoes					
Boots					

CLOSET INVENTORY

Clothing	Have	Need	Colour	Description	Works well with ....
Coats					
Ties					
Jewellery					

Build a simple wardrobe

Women have unlimited options. Again, your career may govern the type of clothing you wear.

Men have four options:

- Suits

- Slacks

- Casual jackets, pants and jeans

- Sweats

You may want to keep your wardrobe simple by wearing classic styles. They can be simple, yet elegant. Build combinations within your wardrobe. Use your closet inventory sheet.

Keep jewellery simple, less is more.

If you need help, check the Yellow Pages for an Image Consultant.

The Kitchen

This is the place and area that everyone uses, so getting organized is the key. First, start going through everything in your freezer and fridge.

The freezer – go through each items and find out if it is marked. Is it dated? Do you know what it is? How long has it been there? Will you ever use it? If not, pass along these items to someone who will. People have a tendency to buy bargains for the freezer, but they never are bargains if you don't use them.

The fridge – again, go through each item. Is it organized? Is any item out of date? Will you ever use it? Are the leftovers sitting there ready to walk? Give the fridge a good cleaning and instruct everyone in the house to keep it that way.

Go through each drawer and cupboard. Measure and buy organizers if needed.

Those things you use on a regular basis, keep close at hand. Other items that are not used as frequently, place in the cupboard on higher shelves.

Do you have two of everything? Why? Keep the best items for yourself. Treat yourself each day like the first class citizen that you are.

How many dinner sets, glasses, pots and pans do you have? How many dinner parties or family functions do you give each year? One lady I know, got rid of her extra stuff and now rents from a party plan company when she is giving a dinner party. The company supplies everything and in some cases, you don't even have to wash it. All items can be returned in the plastic boxes supplied. Enjoy the party and don't worry.

Cookbooks – do you use them? If you don't, pass them along to family and friends. Photocopy those special recipes that you use and like.

Canned goods and packaged items – check the expiry dates: if passed throw it out. If it is stuff you may not use, parcel it up and give it to the food banks. Remember, if an item has no value or purpose to you, pass it along to someone who will value it.

Perhaps you have changed your eating habits. If you have items you will not use, pass them on. If you have three or four of the same items, but in different sizes, keep the medium or large size and sell or give away the other items. In class, I encourage students to bring a list of items that they want to sell, barter, or exchange.

Best china – has to be washed. Has it been in the family for years and you will never use it? Perhaps it looks good in the china cabinet. Why not pass it on to another family member. Give them the responsibility and make sure you arrange for visiting rights.

Often, other family members do not want your stuff for whatever reason. Do you really want to keep it, or perhaps turn it into cash for your travelling fund. Think about it!

Check the yellow pages and you will find that there are some stores that will either sell, find or replace china of certain patterns or designs. One lady I know funded her trip to Europe by selling her china.

Overstuffed drawers and cupboards create high blood pressure and sometimes anger when trying to find something.

The answer: Get organized, pare down and simplify.

Now that you are on a roll, go through each room and simplify, simplify, simplify. Ask yourself the following question when you are looking at each item: "Does this have value and purpose in my life?" If you answer yes, then keep it, otherwise let it go. Simple, don't you think?

Shelf Life of Goods

Food Item, Unopened	Shelf Life
Baking chocolate, chocolate chips	1 year
Bread crumbs	6 months
Cake mix	1 year
Cereal	3 to 4 months
Coffee, canned	1 year
Coffee, instant	6 months
Crackers	3 to 4 months
Evaporated milk	1 year
Fish, canned	2 to 5 years
Flour	1 year
Frosting, canned or dry mix	8 months
Fruits, canned	12 to 18 months
Gelatin	18 months
Gravy, canned	1 year
Herbs, dried	6 months
Honey	1 year
Jams and jellies	1 year
Meat, canned	2 to S years
Nonfat dry milk	6 months
Nuts, shelled	1 month
Olive oil	3 months
Olives	1 year
Onions	2 weeks in the dark
Pasta	1 year
Parmesan cheese, grated	4 months

Food Item, Unopened	Shelf Life
Peanut butter	6 months
Pickles	1 year
Pie-crust mix	8 months
Potatoes	2 weeks in the dark
Pudding mix	1 year
Soft drinks	3 months
Soup, canned	1 year
Soup, dried mix	6 months
Spices, dried, ground	6 months to 1 year
Spices, whole	1 year
Steak sauces	2 years
Sugar, granulated	2 years
Sweetened condensed milk	1 year
Syrup, pancake	1 year
Tabasco sauce	2 years
Tea bags	6 months
Tea, instant	1 year
Tea, loose	6 months
Tomatoes, canned	12 to 18 months
Tomato sauce	1 year
Vegetable oil	3 months
Vegetables, canned	2 to 5 years

Note: You can use these foods past their optimal time frame, but their flavours will fade or textures may be affected.

Living Room

Ask yourself the following questions:

- What's working?
- What's not working?
- What items are essential to you?
- What do you want to get organized?
- What's causing the problem?
- What do you use your living room for?
- Is it for...
- ... family, games or leisure?
- ... TV or music?
- ... napping?
- ... entertaining?

Be creative. Rearrange the furniture if necessary. What can go? What will stay? Draw a floor plan of the living room and rearrange your stuff on the plan. This will give you some idea as to what it will look like.

Storage Space

Sketch your floor plan for each room or space. Come up with a master storage plan worksheet. Remember, you may have to change items several times before you are happy. Consider getting rid of some of your furniture or move it to another room.

Ask yourself what is the cause of the clutter problems. Ask yourself what you want. Is it better access to my belongings? Room to put my guests' coats?

Limited space can often be a major problem. You need to rethink the space that you have and how you can improve things. Check things out before you spend money on space savers and then discover that they do not fit or are too big or small for what you need.

Find a home for everything and I mean everything. Assign a specific function to each closet or drawer. See the example below. Look at the space you have in your clothes closet. Is it possible to move the rod and install two, one lower and the other higher? Could you place a dresser drawer in your closet? Use the back of the door for robes, pyjamas and men's ties. If you have shelving, plastic or wicker baskets can hold socks, underwear and T-shirts. In other words, rethink your space!

Sorting:

Clothes can be sorted by garment. Accessories can be sorted by season. They can also be sorted by category such as belts, scarves, ties or shoes.

Is it for work, dressy, causal or sports?

If it has not been worn in the last year, then let it go!

If you have no eye for colour or style use an Image Consultant (check the Yellow Pages)

Household items can be sorted by category such as light bulbs, tools, adhesives, paper goods, and toiletries.

Linens can be organised by size, set, colour or pattern.

Remember, old clothing can be used for painting, gardening or working on the car or boat. Always consider treating yourself to the first class person that you are. Finally, if you hate clearing your clutter, find it boring or just don't have the time, consider hiring a Clutter Consultant. Good luck!

Making Space Functional

Declutter action plan for the house.

Location	Function of Room	Clutter Problem	Priority	Action Plan	Start / End Date
Entryway					
Living Room					
Family Room					
Den / Home Office					
Kitchen					
Closets / Cabinets					
Bedroom 1					
Bedroom 2					
Attic / Basement					
Garage					
Other					

Instructions:
1. Determine the function of each room (include closets and cabinets).
2. Prioritize by determining which room is currently in the most ineffective, unfunctional state.
3. De-clutter by using boxes and a list method.
4. Schedule a date for a deep clean and a de-clutter assault. One room, one hour at a time.
5. Stop at the end of the time allotted. Enjoy the rest of your day!

Maximize Your Storage Space

Complete this section by using a check mark for the items that either have several homes or have no home at all.

Item	No Home	Have Home	Item	No Home	Have Home
Clothing — Hanging			Serving Pieces		
Clothing — Folded			Groceries		
Coats & Outerwear			Cleaning Supplies		
Shoes			Pet Supplies		
Bags			Stuff to go?		
Jewellery			Dry Cleaning		
Toiletries			Laundry		
Linens			Mail / Packages		
Blankets			Recyclables		
Luggage					
Holiday Decorations			**Other items: (list)**		
Files					
Books					
Collections					
Memorabilia					
Photo Albums					
Records / CDs / Tapes					
Sports Equipment					
Toys					
Games					
Hobby / Craft Supplies					
Gifts (to give)					
Repairs					
Utility / Hardware Dishes					
Glasses					
Flatware					
Pots and Pans					

Use this list in order that you can take positive action to reorganize your life.

Speed Clean Your Home

A great book by Jeff Campbell from Dell Publishing is called *Speed Cleaning*. Jeff explains how to speed clean a house of 1200 square feet in just under one hour.

My suggestion:

Once a month have a real good go at cleaning. Move things, clean under things. So what if you have a little dust here and there? If your friends judge you by this, perhaps you need to change your friends.

Things to toss:

- Junk mail.
- Expired coupons.
- Outdated schedules.
- Old greeting cards – unless they contain special messages or words.
- Old grocery receipts.
- Invitations to past events.
- Expired warranties or service contracts.
- Instructions for items you no longer have.
- Expired insurance policies.
- Unread magazines.
- Old catalogues.
- Investments or banking brochures you never read.
- Cancelled cheques, unless they are needed for tax purposes.
- Old cheque books.
- Receipts for non-tax deductible items.
- Business cards of people you don't recognize.

- Old tourist brochures.
- Outdated road maps.
- Solicitations from charities.
- Recipes you haven't tried in five years.
- Bad quality photos.
- Articles or clippings you haven't read, or reread in more than five years and never will.

Books

You need to carefully go through each book. Have you read it? Will you reread it? If you have never read it, will you? Why are you keeping it?

Books out of date, never been read, read years ago or no plan to read them, pass them along. Create your own *Book of the Month* club and mail books to your family and friends.

I like to recycle my books and share with others. I often pass on my books to friends and give them as gifts. Learn to share as it always comes from the heart.

Donate. You can pass on your books and magazines to any of the following:

- Family
- Friends
- Hospitals
- Doctors offices
- Charities
- Churches
- Senior Citizen Homes
- Hospices

If you want to make some money, rent a table at a flea market. Books are always something people will buy.

Sorting Your Books by:

Size.   Subject.   Author. Hardback versus Paperback.

I like to keep a master log of all of my books. This includes: the name of the book, author, publisher, date and edition. Also, keep a log of all your CD's, video's, and DVD's.

Collectibles (All Around the House)

Do you collect spoons, plates, teddy bears, photos, and cards?

Spoons – have a spoon rack made and display it in an area of the house that you use and is special to you. Remember, value and purpose.

Plates – can be dust collectors. You can still display them and share them with others. If you have moved on from collecting plates, pass them on to a family member, friend or sell them.

Teddy bears, dolls and Beanie Bears – share these fun toys with others. Have a special place or home for them.

Cards and letters – what value or purpose do they have? Are the memories happy or sad ones? Is it time to let go? Only you can truthfully answer those questions.

Photographs – I personally feel they should be shared. They give a story about you, your family and your life. Photo albums are great to use, but are they organized? How often do you look through them?

My suggestions:

Frame pictures and place them around the house. Have a feature wall of the family.

Place pictures under glass. Coffee tables and end tables can have cut glass to fit on top of them so you can place photographs underneath, or in a tray. This can also act as a great conversational piece.

Check stores for new screen frames. Screen frames allow you to display your photographs. Spin frames and iron floor screen frames allow you to also display your photographs.

Creative Memories is a US company with independent consultants in many countries. They supply the know-how and special albums that allow you to journal in it. Great for gifts.

What to do with duplicate or old photographs?

My suggestions:

Duplicate photos – either pass them along to those people that are in the photograph, or make up your own mini photo albums and them give them as a gift. If you want, you can write up details of the event, place and date, if you know it, and include it in the album.

Old photographs – you can use these as gift tags. Place them on the gift, which is especially useful at Christmas. Place them under the tree and let each person find themselves on their gift. It's fun and an opportunity to share their story.

Make your own photo tree – great at Christmas. Place photos, either old, new or make copies of the ones that you have either by colour or black and white copying, or by using a scanner. You can make your own frames and then hang them on the tree. It's different and a great conversational piece.

Photographs are for sharing. They can bring people closer together, give history and a background. They should be out in the open and not kept in a shoe box hidden in the cupboard. Try it, it could be fun!

Cut Your Grocery Shopping in Half

Try to shop once a week, unless you want to go out each day. Some people enjoy shopping daily just to get out of the house and to socialize.

Lump errands together. Plan. Write a list of everything you need before you go. Break this list down by the store. For example, Safeway, Browns', the cleaners and the Post Office.

Buy in bulk and check the flyers: This may save you money.

If you can, plan your meals. Make extra portions, place in small containers and freeze. These meals will be ready for you when you are too tired after a difficult day at work.

Laundry

What happened to washday Mondays? Now we seem to wash everyday. Do we make things last? Wear clothing only once? Won't wear clothing if there are creases? Do we create work?

On a weekly basis, assign towels and face cloths to each member of the household. If they need more, they can get them.

Save time in sorting clothing. Use one laundry basket for dark items another for whites and one for hand-washed pieces. If you have children, give each person their own laundry bag.

Stop buying clothes that need to be dry cleaned, unless it is truly necessary for your image or work. Ask yourself how much you spend per month on dry cleaning.

Do not put things you have worn, once or more, back into your regular closet. Have a separate place. Your clothes will hold smoke, toxins. It's best to air them out, even hanging them in the bathroom.

Extra things to-do to save work

Leave your shoes at the front door (like we used to). Wear slippers or slipper socks. Don't walk mud or dirt through the house.

Go for patterned carpets. Plain carpets show every spec, fleck, dog and cat hair. Use an area carpet over wall-to-wall carpeting. Consider multicolored Persian or oriental rugs where they show less.

If you do not eat each day at your dining room table, then eat from a tray. Accidents do happen - like spaghetti on the carpets!

Houseplants and the garden

Both of these areas take work. If you don't have the time, consider hiring someone, otherwise, it might be time to downsize.

If you do not have a green thumb, consider rubber plants or artificial ones. There are great imitation plants now available.

Lawns need care and attention. No time? Consider hiring a senior or retired person, now moved from their home and living in a flat or apartment. They would love to do some gardening for you, perhaps you can give them their own patch of gardening in return.

If you travel, who will look after your garden? I mean truly look after it?

Simplify if you do not have the time, energy or the money.

Pets

Pets will not simplify your life.

With pets, you will have, veterinarian bills, animal hair all over the place, pulled or torn clothing, marked or ruined furniture and shoes, you will have to exercise and walk them, ...

Pets are for life and need love and attention just as a human beings do.

Take a good look at your lifestyle. Do you travel a great deal? Are you away on the weekend? Is coming home late in the evening a pattern? Do you live in a small home?

If the answer is yes to these questions, then perhaps you need to re-think getting a pet.

Moving

If you are considering moving, sort out and clear your clutter before you move, don't take it with you. When you have decided what to take with you, mark each box clearly with the contents, or use a recorder. Number each box and clearly mark where they are to go. Use a colour code system.

Example:

All blue-marked boxes are for the kitchen, red-marked are for the main living room, yellow-mark are for the master bedroom, black-marked can be designated for the bathroom. Make a master list of this colour code system.

If you are using professional movers or friends, let them know of your colour code system.

Moving is a great opportunity to downsize and rid yourself of stuff you never used or wanted. Have a garage sale or pass items on to friends and charities.

Recycling

Use water filters instead of buying bottled water.

Cut back or eliminate...

- ...daily newspapers, instead get free ones.

- ...magazines, do you read them? Cut back or share subscriptions.

- ...junk mail, stop it. It is just as easy as placing a "No Junk Mail, Please" sticker on or inside your mailbox.

- ...recycle newsprint, mix papers, cardboard, metal cans, plastic containers and glass bottles. Start one in your area.

Recycle gifts (re-gifting). Just remember who gave them to you in the first place. So often we are given things we don't want. Pass these items on to someone that can truly use them.

55 Hot Recycling Hints
KITCHEN:
1. Keep a list so you only buy what you really need.
2. Buy everything you can from bulk bins – it eliminates packaging and can save you money.
3. Buy products such as detergents and cleansers in concentrated form.
4. Take cloth bags to the store or, if you only buy a few items, don't use a bag.
5. Check out consumer magazines before purchasing a major appliance.
6. Compost fruit, vegetable peelings, coffee grounds and tea bags.
7. Store leftover food in old margarine or yogurt tubs instead of plastic wrap and foil.
8. Think litter-less lunches for work or school. Place sandwiches, snacks and drinks in reusable plastic containers. Pack everything into a reusable fabric bag or plastic lunch kit.
9. Reuse aluminum pie plates as freezer containers for baked goods or berries.
10. Line your pots and pans cupboard with scraps of carpet or linoleum to prevent scraping and to reduce noise.

CLOTHES CLOSET:
11. Leftover legs from making denim cutoffs? Sew the bottoms shut to make gift bags or storage bags.
12. Put a sponge inside an old pantyhose leg – they're great for scrubbing dirt from windows and think of all the paper towel you're saving.
13. Mend or alter clothes instead of throwing them away.
14. Take unwanted, good quality clothes to consignment stores or donate to charity.
15. Return extra clothes hangers to a dry cleaner or donate to charity.

BED AND BATH:
16. Look for cosmetics and personal care products with minimal packaging and buy refillables.
17. Use an electric shaver (save on shaving cream/gel). If you prefer a wet shave, buy shaving soap (no container). Buy razors with replacement blades rather than disposables.
18. Cut up old towels and bed linens and use them for household chores such as dusting. You can also donate them to an animal shelter for pet bedding.
19. Use old toothbrushes as cleaning tools for those hard to reach places.
20. Use an old shower curtain as a drop cloth when painting or as a ground sheet for camping.

LIVING ROOM / FAMILY ROOM:
21. Borrow books from the library or buy them second-hand. Share subscriptions with a friend or neighbour. Once read, pass them on or donate.
22. Check consumer magazines BEFORE buying a new TV or stereo.
23. Buy used CD's and tapes. Sell or donate those you no longer want.
24. Cover favourite books with used maps, posters, gift wrap or fabric – they'll last longer.

25. Donate old photographic equipment to schools to use in art classes or for their newspapers.
26. Make new furniture from old, become resourceful, imaginative.:
    1. An ashtray stand becomes a plant holder
    2. An old trunk finds new life as a coffee table, complete with storage
27. Donate your old furniture to charity or a theatre company or, give it a facelift by repainting, refinishing or restoring it.

HOME OFFICE:
28. Paper printed on one side? Reuse it for drafts, make note pads or use the blank side for incoming faxes.
29. Buy paper with recycled content, also look for products packaged with recycled materials.
30. Re-label old file folders and re-use them.
31. Save old envelopes and re-use them. You can even write, "this envelop was re-used in the spirit of recycling".

SHED / GARAGE:
32. Rent or borrow items that are only used occasionally.
33. Renovating your house? Buy salvaged materials like sinks, flooring and dimensional lumber.
34. Buy nails, screws and other necessities in bulk. Store them in old glass jars.
35. Spring cleaning? Have a yard sale, your trash may be someone else's treasure!
36. Leaky hose? Add more holes with a flat nail and use as a soaker hose to water your flowers or garden.

SPECIAL OCCASIONS / CELEBRATIONS:
37. Having a large get-together? Instead of purchasing disposables, rent dishes, etc. or have guests bring their own.
38. Create unique floral vases:
    1. Use an old watering can or teapot that's lost its lid.

2. Use a cluster of small jars or hollow out a
watermelon or pumpkin and fill with flowers /
leaves, etc.
39. Make your own gift wrap by being creative.
Sometimes, just a ribbon and a bow is all a gift
needs. Reduce, Re-use, Recycle and REJOICE!

PACKAGING:
40. Buy larger sizes. As packages get bigger, you
get more product and proportionately less
packaging.
41. Use plastic bags for fruits and vegetables
sparingly. Bananas and other produce come in
their own natural packaging.
42. Buy refillable containers and refills. Refills
reduce garbage.
43. Check your options for purchasing unpackaged
items;
1. Buy a shirt from a hanger instead of a
package.
2. Say 'No' to extra tissue wrap (unless you have
a need for it).
3. Leave the boot box at the store.
44. Avoid over-packaged items such as a box within
a box, unless you feel you MUST have it or you
have a need for the 'extra' box.
45. Buy light bulbs in boxes of two or more. You'll
reduce the amount of packaging per bulb and
likely save money too.
46. Re-use ice cream pails to pick berries, freeze
cookies, sort odds and ends, or to collect fruit
and vegetable trimmings for composting.
47. Fill handled 4-litre jugs with water and freeze as
part of your emergency preparedness plan.
48. Turn empty cereal boxes into handy recycling
boxes. Just cut off the top and decorate. Or cut
the box on the diagonal to make a container for
file folders or magazines.
49. Use egg cartoons to sort beads, buttons, nails
and other small objects, or for starting seeds.
50. Create piggy banks out of milk jugs. Turn milk
cartons, jugs and margarine tubs into bird
feeders.

51. Use old shoe boxes to pack a travel kit with crayons, recycled scratch pads and other children's activities or to store holiday decorations, sewing notions, etc.
52. Use reusable containers for all your tidbits:
    1. Used pill bottles for salt and pepper, or paper clips and other small items.
    2. An ice cream pail for potato salad.
    3. Yogurt tubs for vegetable and dip
    4. Gable-topped milk or juice cartons filled with water and frozen for ice packs.
53. Pack ice cubes in a double-bagged shopping bag. The ice cubes will keep food fresh and drinks cool.
54. Pack your beach stuff in a large empty detergent box or pail with carrying handles (or use it around the house for storage).
55. Buy a gift for the CONTENTS, not the glitzy packaging.

CLUTTER ACTION PLAN: REVIEW AND SELF-EVALUATION

Name: _____

Week of: _____ / _____

         From   To

☐ **Household**   ☐ **Career**   ☐ **Health**

☐ **Lifestyle**   ☐ **Finances**   ☐ **Relationships**

1. **AREAS I WORKED ON THIS WEEK: List the SUCCESSES** that you have had this week. A success might be a project that you started or completed.

_____

_____

_____

_____

Did you remember to REWARD yourself at the end of each job/project completed?
Suggestion: Set a timeline for each item.

2. **AREAS I WILL WORK ON THIS COMING WEEK:** List projects that you wish to start or completed in the coming week. They are:

_____

_____

_____

_____

3. Remember to complete your CLUTTER ACTION PLAN each week.
4. Do not do zig-zag de-cluttering. Complete ONE task at a time BEFORE moving to the next one.
5. Give yourself a pat on the back, take a break and remember to REWARD YOURSELF (something consumable, breakfast, dinner, a bottle of wine, or a movie, massage or something "FUN")
6. A final word: Remember, Rome was not built in a day and your clutter will not disappear overnight. Be good to yourself, pace yourself and have patience.
GOOD LUCK!

Talbot's Tips

- Your goal is to make cleaning as easy as possible, but if you do not like it, try and make it FUN. Play some music and turn it into a form of exercise. Set a timer and go for it!

- Use the organizing principle "Group Like Things Together": this will save you time and energy searching.

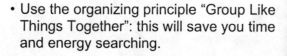

YOUR LIFESTYLE

Your lifestyle will determine the clothes you have and need, the car you drive and perhaps even where and how you live. Do you entertain a great deal?

Is downsizing the answer? Can you move to a small place? Do you need three bedrooms? Are two never used except when the kids come home?

Is there financial burden where you are now living? Are you trying to keep up with the Jones'?

If you are self-employed or freelance, can you work from home?

Savings would include:

- Clothing

- Transportation

- Lunches and meals

- Time

Can you work alone and from home? Would you want to? Can you discipline yourself? What are your options?

Reduce your go-go entertainment

Many people are never home to enjoy their home. They are out, hitting the nightlife, or actively involved with too many groups or associations and then wonder why they are always tired and never able to get together with friends.

My suggestions:

- Cut back on your nightlife, if you want to.

- Take a hard look at those associations you belong to. What do you get out of it and what do you contribute?

- Have people in for potluck suppers.

- Share or split food if you are out or at home.

- Rotate potluck suppers. It's a great way to see friends on a regular basis.

- Rotate at different restaurants with friends or a partner. Make it a treat, no cooking or washing up!

ENJOY!

85 Things That You Can do

1. Plan your TV time, be more selective. Consider turning off your TV, unplugging it, or even covering it.

2. Make a cover for the TV.

3. Read a book, poem or play.

4. Talk with a friend, relative or neighbour. Have them over.

5. Sing a song, play music or play an instrument.

6. Bake cookies.

7. Visit an elderly person.

8. Volunteer locally.

9. Clean the garage.

10. Spend time in the natural world.

11. Play a game with children.

12. Write a letter. Write in your journal.

13. Look through old photo albums

14. Tell a family story.

15. Go on a picnic

16. Take time to really explore your library.

17. Go on a date.

18. Plant a tree or flowers.

19. Prepare a garden for spring.

20. Go swimming.

21. Make a pizza from scratch.

22. Visit the library (for the recipe).

23. Draw a picture.

24. Tape your picture to the refrigerator door.

25. Clean the refrigerator.

26. Soak in a hot bath for a long time. Plan quiet time for you: bath, facemask, massage, nails.

27. Call Grandma, or someone special.

28. Stretch.

29. Balance your chequebook.

30. Help your kids with their homework.

31. Go to sleep early.

32. Take the snow tires off of the car.

33. Write a poem, story, song or essay.

34. Give your pet a bath.

35. Play with your pets.

36. Listen to music.

37. Learn a new skill.

38. Start with a family genealogy chart.

39. Look under the sofa cushions for spare change.

40. Reread your journal.

41. Fast.

42. Meditate.

43. Wash the car.

44. Enjoy the silence of your living room.

45. Borrow old radio programs from the library.

46. Listen to a contemporary radio show (something that is different).

47. Shovel snow off the walk, driveway or roof.

48. Make something with the kids (cooking or art project).

49. Dust the house.

50. Host a neighbourhood potluck.

51. Exercise.

52. Leave the house to explore new areas of your neighbourhood or town by foot.

53. Build a fire, make tea and just be in the here and now.

54. Go to a high school sporting event.

55. Have a candlelight dinner with a loved one.

56. Play cribbage or a game with friends – if you don't know, learn.

57. Build a treehouse.

58. Start a compost pile.

59. Sign up to take or teach a community education class.

60. Start your winter holiday and Christmas cards.

61. Make candles

62. Learn something new.

63. Make root beer.

64. Learn to identify ten plants in your area.

65. Chop wood.

66. Make a bird feeder or birdhouse and put them in your yard.

67. Learn ten birds that visit your feeder.

68. Shine your shoes or boots.

69. Walk your dog or someone else's.

70. Make a gift for someone.

71. Organize your closet.

72. Donate unused clothing to a charity.

73. Test the battery in your smoke detector and replace it if necessary.

74. Learn how to recycle.

75. Reread the book *"Your Money or Your Life."*

76. Write a letter to a politician or local newspaper on issues that you are concerned about.

77. Start a saving account.

78. Go to the park. Go to a museum or art gallery.

79. Check out books about the effects and history of television from your local library.

80. Carve a walking stick from a piece of driftwood or fallen branch.

81. Start a dream notebook (often called a wishbook).

82. Sell or give away your TV so you can revisit this list every week thereafter.

83. Do jigsaw puzzles.

84. Have a video night with friends.

85. Start a book club.

Stop call waiting – I HATE IT!

How many times have you been put on hold while talking to a friend and they suddenly say, "Can you please hold, I have another call coming". I personally feel that we get enough of this during our business day. This I accept, but not at home. Unless someone tells me that they are expecting a special call or a long distance call, then I expect them to give me their full attention. Otherwise they can call me when they have time to chat.

Use your answering machine to screen your calls. Block off time to return all calls. Learn to use your time more efficiently and effectively. Don't answer the phone when you are sitting down eating. Let the machine pick it up. Eat, enjoy and then return your phone calls.

Don't answer the door unless you are expecting someone and always check via the peephole. Make sure you have a chain on your inside door, especially if you live alone.

Do you really need car phones and cell phones, or are you trying to keep up with everyone else?

Holidays

Holidays can be stressful and expensive. If you don't want to go, stay home. Don't tell anyone. Do the things that you want to do like visit the local museums.

See the section 'Take a Vacation at Home' on page 85.

Holidays should be fun! Everyone should be involved with organizing it and helping to pack. Make it a family or friend holiday.

Lay out on the bed all the things that you will need and then halve the items. Be ruthless. Are you going on holiday or a fashion show?

See the section, 'Travelling Simplified' on page 87. Holidays should be carefree and fun!

Sometimes going on holiday alone is the best thing you can do for you.

If it doesn't feel right, change it, or don't do it.

Take a vacation at home

Refer back to the section, '*Holidays*' on page 85. First, don't tell friends that this holiday will be at home, unless you want to. Otherwise the phone will be constantly ringing and defeat the purpose of your vacation.

Things you can do:

• Nothing

• Work on your clutter.

• Read a good book.

• Get the house in order.

• Paint, decorate or clean.

• Visit local art galleries and museums. It would be something you would never do unless you have out-of-town visitors.

• Go on a coach tour. Be a tourist in your own city or town.

• Spoil yourself, go to a posh restaurant.

• Book into a hotel, often they have midweek specials.

• Visit a spa. Spoil yourself and have a massage, manicure, pedicure, facial or reflexology.

• Get your hair done and perhaps a new colour. It will give you a new look.

• Go on a picnic.

• Rent movies or all those taped movies and shows that you never had time to watch.

• Buy a box of chocolates, a bottle of wine or popcorn.

• Start or write a journal.

• Sip coffee or cappuccino in an outdoor coffeehouse while you read a newspaper, journal, or magazine.

• Take yourself out for breakfast.

• Walk your dog, or someone else's, in the park.

• Take your camera out and photograph whatever strikes you.

• Take a course, something that you have always wanted to do.

In other words, spoil yourself. Do something special for you, you're worth it!

Travelling simplified

• Wear and take only dark coloured clothing that won't show the dirt and it's easy to manage.

• Make a list of all that you will need for your trip or special events attending.

• Take clothes that don't wrinkle easily.

• Mix and match – how many outfits can you get from the basics, taking into account the things you will be doing?

• Wear things that you can hand wash, take your own travel line to hang in the bathroom.

• Take a travel iron and adapter.

• Bring a toilet bag with small sample-type items. Leave the family size at home unless the family is travelling with you.

Place all the items on the bed. Usually if you can cut in half the items you are taking, you will have more than enough.

Roll your clothes in tissue paper so they won't wrinkle and you can pack more into a smaller space.

If possible, try to use only carry-on luggage. This will save time at the airport. In your hand luggage, pack your papers, passport, small toilet bag with everything and even clean underwear. If your bag gets lost, you are still all right for the first day or so. (Nowadays, it is strongly suggested to check with your airline as to the current luggage security-related allowance.)

Gift giving simplified

Stop giving. Instead, tell your family and friends that you are giving to a charity.

Buy all year round. When you see it, buy it. Keep a list of all purchases and whom they are for. Go to church or craft fairs. Unusual gifts for gift giving are often found there.

Learn to make it. This can be a new hobby or an old one revisited.

Keep a place for all your gifts. I have a box that I keep everything in.

Cards – buy them in bulk or learn to make your own (I did!). At the start of each month, I write up all my cards and put the date in the right hand corner where the stamp will be placed.

Christmas cards – stop sending them if it doesn't feel right.

Make and create your own newsletter. I do mine twice a year for the summer and Christmas. This way, it keeps me in touch with friends on a regular basis.

Unless you have the time and you truly love letter writing, then a newsletter is a great and easy way to keep in touch with those you love.

One friend that I have sends her newsletter in January. She says that is usually a 'down' month for people and the newsletter gives them something to look forward to.

Drive a simpler car

Do you need a car? Must it be new, or would a second-hand car be enough?

See the section called 'Finances' on cars (page 105). Check costs for insurance, taxes, gas or petrol and maintenance.

Do you need your car for work and for pleasure? Use a car-share program. Check your local directory.

CLUTTER ACTION PLAN: REVIEW AND SELF-EVALUATION

Name: _____

Week of: _____ / _____
          From   To

☐ **Household**   ☐ **Career**   ☐ **Health**
☐ **Lifestyle**   ☐ **Finances**   ☐ **Relationships**

1. **AREAS I WORKED ON THIS WEEK:** List the SUCCESSES that you have had this week. A success might be a project that you started or completed.

_____

_____

_____

_____

Did you remember to REWARD yourself at the end of each job/project completed?
Suggestion: Set a timeline for each item.

2. **AREAS I WILL WORK ON THIS COMING WEEK:** List projects that you wish to start or completed in the coming week. They are:

_____

_____

_____

_____

3. Remember to complete your CLUTTER ACTION PLAN each week.
4. Do not do zig-zag de-cluttering. Complete ONE task at a time BEFORE moving to the next one.
5. Give yourself a pat on the back, take a break and remember to REWARD YOURSELF (something consumable, dinner, a bottle of wine, breakfast, or a movie, massage or something "FUN")
6. A final word: Remember, Rome was not built in a day and your clutter will not disappear overnight. Be good to yourself, pace yourself and have patience.
                    GOOD LUCK!

Talbot's Tips

- Plan a minimum of two hours
  per week to work on
  your clutter.

- Perhaps 15 minutes per day will
  be enough for you, or you may wish
  to do 30 to 60 minutes. In other words...
  PACE YOURSELF.

Your Health

Having personally experienced major surgery November 1998 for cancer and spending most of 1999 recovering, I know how important health is.

Here are some suggestions:

- Simplify your eating habits.

- Watch your diet, obtain expert advice if necessary.

- If possible, plan your meals for the week. Many people eat junk food and quick snacks just because they are too busy.

- Learn to cook simple meals like homemade soups. Freeze soups and pastas in small containers so that a meal is ready in a moment. Invest in a good cookbook that will give you ideas and inexpensive meals to cook and freeze.

- If necessary, take a cooking class. It's fun and you learn how to cook. You get to eat what you produce and you meet new people.

- Eat fresh fruit daily.

- Salads are great at any time and they take very little effort.

- Drink 8 to 10 glasses of water each day. This was difficult for me before going into the hospital, but they would make you drink this amount of water to flush the toxins out of your body. This is a must!

- Don't overeat. If necessary, split a restaurant meal or a dessert.

- Fast one day a week. First check with your doctor, especially if you have a medical problems.

- What are you drinking? Is it too much coffee, tea, wine or spirits?

- Bake your own muffins as they will be cheaper, healthier and good for you when you use oat, bran or similar ingredients. There are some great cookbooks on muffins, bread and other baked goods.

- Pack your lunch two to three times a week. This will help you save money and have a healthy and safe way to control what you eat. When you eat out, then it is a real treat to enjoy and have fun.

What kind of exercise do you do?

Do you have exercise equipment, but never use it? You have paid a good price for it and now the equipment sits there, gathering dust. Consider selling, bartering or trading it for something you really want.

Fire your personal trainer unless this is the only way you can exercise. Instead, go for a walk, jog or run and find a buddy to do it with.

Get up an hour earlier in the morning, just for you. Be in bed by 9pm one night a week, just for you.

Remember, no books or phone calls. Learn to relax and do nothing.

Create your own rituals

Find a special place in your home, just for you. It can be a chair or even a place by the window.

This is a place where you can drink your own special tea in your own special cup. It's a place to read or write up your own daily journal. Or it can be a place to meditate, rest, close your eyes and relax. In other words, it's a place where you can spoil yourself.

Learn to laugh

How often do you laugh?

Research tells us that children laugh 20 to 40 time a day, but when we are an adult, we laugh only four to eight times a day.

The question is, "Why do we laugh less as an adult?" Is life that stressful?

Learn yoga. Local community centres and night classes have details and costs.

Learn to meditate. It takes time for some people, but a great way to relax and slow down in the fast pace we live in.

Take time to watch the sunset. In other words, stop and smell the roses.

CLUTTER ACTION PLAN: REVIEW AND SELF-EVALUATION

Name: _____

Week of: _____ / _____
            From   To

☐ **Household**   ☐ **Career**   ☐ **Health**
☐ **Lifestyle**   ☐ **Finances**   ☐ **Relationships**

1. AREAS I WORKED ON THIS WEEK: List the SUCCESSES that you have had this week. A success might be a project that you started or completed.

_____

_____

_____

_____

Did you remember to REWARD yourself at the end of each job/project completed?
Suggestion: Set a timeline for each item.

2. AREAS I WILL WORK ON THIS COMING WEEK: List projects that you wish to start or completed in the coming week. They are:

_____

_____

_____

_____

3. Remember to complete your CLUTTER ACTION PLAN each week.
4. Do not do zig-zag de-cluttering. Complete ONE task at a time BEFORE moving to the next one.
5. Give yourself a pat on the back, take a break and remember to REWARD YOURSELF (something consumable, dinner, a bottle of wine, breakfast, or a movie, massage or something "FUN")
6. A final word: Remember, Rome was not built in a day and your clutter will not disappear overnight. Be good to yourself, pace yourself and have patience.
GOOD LUCK!

YOUR RELATIONSHIPS

With:

• Partner(s)

• Family

• Friends

• Co-workers

Ask yourself, what you are getting out of the relationship. What are you putting into it and what is the other person putting into it at the same time. If you cannot be yourself with your family and friends and you have to pretend, is this truly living your life? Just be yourself each and everyday of your life.

Trust your intuition. That sixth sense is a gut feeling and is often the best. Check out the book *Practical Intuition*, by Laura Day, available in both paper and hardback.

If it is not easy, then just don't do it. What are you trying to prove?

Stop trying to change people and accept them as they are, just as you want them to accept you.

Spend one day a month in solitude. This can be difficult for some people to do the first time, but after that, it is a great way to shut out the world as we know it, and recharge our batteries.

Teach your kids the joy of solitude.

Do a retreat once a year, invest in you.

Keep a journal or a gratitude book.

Start your own wish book, not only for yourself, but include others too.

If you cannot multi-task, then learn to do one thing at a time and do it well.

Do nothing. This can be very hard for some people, but it's a wonderful way to relax, breathe in, reflect and be grateful for all you have in your life.

Go for a walk. It's a great way to exercise with plenty of fresh air, a way of meeting people again and again and to be so thankful to be on this earth.

Play on the beach. Remember the things you did as a kid? Why not do them now as an adult? Let the child in you shine through.

Drink hot chocolate. This is one of my favourite drinks with a blob of cream on top.

Just say no. Again, this can be difficult for many of us, but so often we say yes just to please others at the expense of ourselves.

Resign from any organization whose meetings either you or they have outgrown, or you dread.

Learn to reinterpret the past. We cannot relive it and probably don't want to, but we can learn and grow from it.

Change your expectations of yourself and others.

Review your life regularly to keep it simple.

CLUTTER ACTION PLAN: REVIEW AND SELF-EVALUATION

Name: _____

Week of: _____ / _____

From   To

☐ Household   ☐ Career   ☐ Health
☐ Lifestyle   ☐ Finances   ☐ Relationships

1. AREAS I WORKED ON THIS WEEK: List the SUCCESSES that you have had this week. A success might be a project that you started or completed.

_____

_____

_____

_____

Did you remember to REWARD yourself at the end of each job/project completed?
Suggestion: Set a timeline for each item.

2. AREAS I WILL WORK ON THIS COMING WEEK: List projects that you wish to start or completed in the coming week. They are:

_____

_____

_____

_____

3. Remember to complete your CLUTTER ACTION PLAN each week.
4. Do not do zig-zag de-cluttering. Complete ONE task at a time BEFORE moving to the next one.
5. Give yourself a pat on the back, take a break and remember to REWARD YOURSELF (something consumable, dinner, a bottle of wine, breakfast, or a movie, massage or something "FUN")
6. A final word: Remember, Rome was not built in a day and your clutter will not disappear overnight. Be good to yourself, pace yourself and have patience.
GOOD LUCK!

YOUR FINANCES

- Get yourself out of debt.
- Know your family monthly income.
- Know your family monthly expenses.
- Live on half of what you earn (you can do it, I did).
- Go for debt counselling if your situation is out of control.

Questions to ask yourself about getting organized:

- Do you pay your bills on time?
- Do you stop wasting money on late fees and charges?
- Do you want your dining room table back? Clear the space of clutter and unopened bills that need attention.
- Does all the hideous paper cluttering everything cause tension?
- Do you want to feel more in control instead of always anxious that you are forgetting something?

Zones or areas

Activities	Supplies	Storage Units
Mail and paper flow	Mail inbox	Top kitchen drawer
	Mail outbox	
	Invitations	
	School papers to sign	
	Stationary and cards	
	Envelopes	
	Postage stamps	

You may use the same system as above for paying all of your bills. Keep them altogether, mark your wall calendar for when they have to be paid for. Poor credit can effect your credit rating.

What are your money weaknesses and attitude towards money?

- Do you spend money impulsively?

- Are you excessively frugal?

- Are you a risk-taker with money?

- Do you trust and listen to your financial advisor?

- Do you have a nest egg mentality?

- Do you tend to gamble?

- Do you use money to boost your self-esteem?

- Do you want to exercise excessive control over your money?

- Do you have contempt for money?

It is important to have an accurate account of all your outgoing expenses. It is important to record every penny spent for the last three months (some months may vary as far as expenses are concerned). This will give you a true picture where and how you spend your money.

Once you have committed this to paper, you will have an opportunity to:

- Pay off your debts starting with your credit cards.

- Rethink your buying habits.

- Consider second-hand, rather than new.

- Delay major purchases and shop around asking yourself, do you really need it and could you buy it second-hand.

- Is there an alternative?

- Start paying by cash, debit cards and cheque only, using a credit card only for major purchases.

- Change the way you shop and use the buddy system.

- Establish an emergency fund of three to six months income, depending on your lifestyle.

- What happens if you lost your job today, could you survive and how?

- Get life insurance, a will, power of attorney and disability insurance.

- Invest monthly in RRSP's.

- Invest ten percent of your after tax each month and expect to leave it there for at least ten years.

  Reduce your need for goods and services.

  Consolidate your chequing accounts. Do you have several accounts? Remember that you will pay an administration fee for each one.

  Can and do you balance your account each month? Use the simple check register system. Money in - money out = balance (and include those administration fee and charges!)

Personal budget planner

Personal Statistics	
Name:	Phone Numbers:
Address:	Marital Status:
City, Postal Code:	Dependents:
Occupation:	Employer:
Source(s) of Income	
Principal Monthly Income:	
Secondary Monthly Income:	
Other Income:	**Gross Total: $**
Deductions	
Medical / Dental:	
RRSP / Pension / Union Dues:	**Deduction Total: $**
Income Tax / CPP / EI:	**Net Income Per Cheque: $**
Regular Monthly Expenses	
Rent / Mortgage:	Daycare / School Costs:
Telephone:	Medical / Dental / Optical:
Hydro:	Babysitting / Allowances:
Cable:	Food:
Heat:	Dry Cleaning / Laundry:
Water / Garbage:	Other:
	Monthly Total; $

Annual Payments (Divide by 12)	
Car Insurance:	Travel:
House Insurance:	Gifts:
Rent Insurance:	Clothing:
House Expenses (repairs):	Income Tax:
Christmas:	**Total: $**
Monthly Transportation Costs	
Gas / Oil:	Public Transportation:
Car Repairs:	Taxi:
Parking:	**Total: $**
Entertainment / Personal Care	
Eat Out Work:	Membership Fees:
Eat Out Social:	Course Fees:
Alcohol Out:	Movies / Concerts / Videos:
Liquor Store:	Magazines / Music / Books:
Cigarettes:	Hobbies:
Lottery Pool:	Photo / Film:
Cosmetics / Perfume:	Health Food / Vitamins:
Medication:	Pets / Vet:
Other:	**Total: $**

Are your expenses exceeding your net income?

Credit Cards:

Type	% Rate	Monthly payment	Balance

Total Outstanding Loans: $

Loans:

Type	% Rate	Monthly payment	Balance

Total Outstanding Loans: $

Bank Accounts:

Type	% Rate	Type	Balance

Assets – RRPS's..

Name	% Rate	Due Date	Balance

Other Information

Variable and other expenses

Remember to keep accurate records of your weekly spending before transferring monthly totals to this sheet.

	Jan	Feb	Mar	Apr	May	Jun	Jul	Aug	Sep	Oct	Nov	Dec
Groceries												
Drugs												
Heating (Gas or other)												
Lunch / Eating out												
House Maintenance												
Garden Maintenance												
Furnishings												
Clothes												
Gifts												
Hydro												
Telephone												
Haircuts												
Dry-cleaning												
Misc / Cards / Fabric												
Stamps / Books												
Courses / Fees												
Subscriptions												
Entertainment												
Liquor												
Holidays / Tickets												
Car Maintenance												
Gasoline (Vehicle)												

Investments

Are you truly making money?

Pay for an expert that can help advise you.

Can you afford to lose money?

Pay off your mortgage if you can.

Check details because sometimes penalties do apply. Look at the advantages versus the disadvantages. Get advice, it may be well worth it.

Buying a car

A new car will lose about 30% or more of its value when you drive it off the lot. After two years, the car will lose another 30% from its original price.

Do you have the money for a new car, will you need to finance it?

Do you need a new car due to your job and the fact that you do a great deal of driving every day? Could you buy outright a second-hand car and would it do the job for you?

Teach your kids fiscal responsibility. They will learn that if they do not have the money, they can't afford it. Money does not grow on trees.

Often buying credit can lead to serious financial difficulties.

Your job or career

- Today there is no security of a life-long job.

- Stop being a slave to your day timer.

- Simplify your system.

- If you are controlled by your system, something is wrong.

- Consider working where you live or, live where you work.

- How much time do you spend travelling to and from work each day?

- Is it worth it? Look at the time, the income and the stress.

- Are you doing what you truly, truly want to do?

If you do not feel fulfilled in your present job, perhaps it is time for a change. Talk to your friends, ask them what they feel you would be good at.

Sign up for a job club, vocational and career assessment, or counselling. Do your own research at the library, call companies for which you feel you might want to work. This is called an information interview, you are not asking for a job, you want to know what's involved, the skills needed and required.

Turn your hobby into a job. Many people have done this and there are many books available on such people.

Remember you only have one life to live, live it now! Stop the busy work. Consider working less and enjoying life more. Balance in your life is vital – are you balanced?

Do you...

• ...make unnecessary phone calls?

• ...organize and reorganize your schedule, people, reports and paperwork?

• ...re-do things over and over again?

• ...join groups just to be seen, or is it a must – what do you get from it and what do you give?

What would happen if you did nothing for a day? Could you do nothing?

Remember to include your family in your work life.

Consider:

• Sharing with each person for 15 to 20 minutes.

• Let each person have this opportunity.

• By sharing, this will keep the family together...

• and, by doing this, solutions may arise from this family discussion.

Consult our "Suggested Reading List", the section "Work and Career" on page 147.

Hardcore simplicity

- Minimize your accessories.
- Stop carrying a purse the size of the *Queen Elizabeth II*
- Rent rather than own (your choice).
- Get rid of your cars and simplify.
- Stop making the bed each day.
- Get rid of all the extras.
- Build a very simple wardrobe.
- Find a place for everything.
- Establish homes for commonly used items so you don't waste time looking for them.
- File, don't pile. Paper is the number one source of clutter from junk mail to work documents to personal records.
- Open your mail daily, preferably near a recycling bin.
- Be ruthless. Throw out what you do not need.
- Invest in a simple filing system. Check your local office supply company.
- Finish what you start.
- Procrastination is the enemy of order, so pledge to complete tasks you start.
- Simplify.
- Find a buddy, someone to support, motivate you.
- If you don't have the time or energy, request help or hire someone.

Are you really organized?

The following quiz is designed to help you decide whether your family and home need an organizational overhaul.

- Do you carry a calendar with you at all times?   Y / N
- Do you set priorities? . . . .   Y / N
- Do you make appointments with yourself? . .   Y / N
- Do you put aside time each week to get organized or maintain your organizational system? . . . .   Y / N
- Are you always on time for scheduled appointments? . . . .   Y / N
- Do you have a mail system to avoid misplacing important information? . . . .   Y / N
- Do you use an answering machine or portable phone? . . . .   Y / N
- Do you keep a grocery list and follow it? . . . .   Y / N
- Do the clothes that you keep in your closet fit you? Y/N
- Do you wear them regularly? . . . .   Y / N
- Do all the family members share in household chores? . . . .   Y / N
- Do you store like items together? . . . .   Y / N
- Do you spend less then 30 minutes cleaning up your house at the end of the day? . . . .   Y / N

If you answered "No" more than five times, your quality of live could improve with some organizational tools and guidance.

A daily simplicity checklist

Since living a simpler life means bringing more meaning, more reflection, more gratitude and more of me into my daily experience, I will commit to completing this checklist for 30 days.

- What did I do today that I'm proud of?
- Did I complete anything today?
- Did I do something that leaves me anxious?

- Did I keep a commitment?

- Did I do anything I've been meaning to do for a long time?

- Did I make any decisions today that will improve the quality of my life?

- Did I laugh today? At what?

- Did I spend time with the people I love? Who?

- What unexpected events came my way?

- Did I help anyone today?

- Did anyone help me?

    Your name: . . . .

    Today's date: . . . .

    "Learn to enjoy things without owning them."

Clean Up Your Act Now!

by Paul Talbot

Here are eight steps to creating a home office that is better organized.

1. ***Remove the very obvious trash***

   Take a garbage bag and fill it. Remember to recycle what you can.

2. ***Group similar things together***

   Start by making piles all over the floor to group similar items together. For example: unpaid bills in one pile, paid bills (to be filed) in another, correspondence that needs attention, credit card receipts, project ideas, phone numbers to be placed in you're a-Z, etc.

3. ***Create a "TO DO" list***

   I suggest you use a note pad (keep it handy in one place). Lists will help keep you on track and focussed.

4. ***Don't agonize***

   Make a decision. If you are unsure, think about it overnight and then let it go.

5. ***Get Help***

   Enlist a friend or pay someone to help you. Send out for pizza at the end of the day as a "reward". Get the job done and then move on.

6. ***Put things away***

   Change your old habits. Put things away or hang things up – you will soon notice the difference.

7.   *Don't get sidetracked*

Your "TO DO" list will help keep you on track. Block off time in order to complete certain projects or tasks. Let the answering machine pick up your calls. Later on when you have finished the project/s, return all calls in a 'block'.

8.   *Start on the future*

Write down your goals. Review them on a regular basis. Update your "TO DO" lists. Getting organized is a means to an end. Having a more productive, stress-free work environment means more time for you, your family and friends.

GOOD LUCK!

CLUTTER ACTION PLAN: REVIEW AND SELF-EVALUATION

Name: _____

Week of: _____ / _____

         From   To

☐ **Household**   ☐ **Career**   ☐ **Health**
☐ **Lifestyle**   ☐ **Finances**   ☐ **Relationships**

1. AREAS I WORKED ON THIS WEEK: List the SUCCESSES that you have had this week. A success might be a project that you started or completed.

_____

_____

_____

_____

Did you remember to REWARD yourself at the end of each job/project completed?
Suggestion: Set a timeline for each item.

2. AREAS I WILL WORK ON THIS COMING WEEK: List projects that you wish to start or completed in the coming week. They are:

_____

_____

_____

_____

3. Remember to complete your CLUTTER ACTION PLAN each week.
4. Do not do zig-zag de-cluttering. Complete ONE task at a time BEFORE moving to the next one.
5. Give yourself a pat on the back, take a break and remember to REWARD YOURSELF (something consumable, dinner, a bottle of wine, breakfast, or a movie, massage or something "FUN")
6. A final word: Remember, Rome was not built in a day and your clutter will not disappear overnight. Be good to yourself, pace yourself and have patience.
GOOD LUCK!

Talbot's Tips

- When you take off your clothes, put them in the laundry hamper or hang them in the bathroom to air (if worn only once).

- After showering, hang your towel(s).

Your Career

Clutter at home and in our life can impact and affect our productivity in the workplace, as well as our relationships with our co-workers. This section will highlight the workplace issues that you may encounter in your professional life. Through quizzes and point forms, you will be able to move forward daily.

However, even though you are in charge of your own home and destiny, at work you may have a supervisor or other co-workers with whom you should consult before implementing changes that you feel are necessary.

Teamwork is essential in making any changes as this could result in stress, anxiety, spinning your wheels and loss of sleep.

Clear Your Desk Clutter: Take the Quiz! HOW CLUTTERED IS YOUR DESK?

1. While sitting at your desk, do you feel completely overwhelmed by the backlog of paperwork facing you? Y / N

2. Do you frequently worry about unfinished paperwork on your desk when you are away from the office? Y / N

3. Is there so much paperwork on the desk that you have to find another clear space to tackle another project? Y / N

4. Do you have days in the office when you have been extremely busy dealing with paperwork but don't feel you have achieved anything constructive? Y / N

5. Do you often fill your briefcase with paperwork to deal with at home? Y / N

6. Do you often stay late in the office to try and catch up on the 'backlog'? Y / N

7. Do you spend too much time "fire-fighting" because paperwork has not been dealt with effectively? Y / N

8. While working on one project, are you often distracted by other paperwork around you on your desk? Y / N

9. Do you ever find paperwork on your desk that you have forgotten about and it is too late to do anything with? Y / N

10. Do you spend too much time looking for paperwork on or around your desk? Y / N

11. Do you often put off uncomfortable paperwork and deal with lower pay-off and more interesting items? Y / N

12. Do you sometimes miss important opportunities because you have been too busy to deal with the paperwork? Y / N

13. Do you often handle paperwork several times before finally deciding what to do with it? Y / N

14. Do you face too many interruptions from your colleagues rushing your desk with paperwork for your attention? Y / N

15. Do you always keep paperwork moving? Y / N

SCORE   Yes   0 - 5   You have your paperwork under control.
6 - 10   Most people fit this category. Some improvement is needed.

NAME: _____   DATE: _____

How Effectively Do You Handle Your Priority Paperwork?

1. If asked to find three items of paperwork on your desk which   Y / N
    would lead to the highest pay-off, would you have to search for
    them in different stacks of paper?

2. Do you often plan to tackle certain items of paperwork on the   Y / N
    desk but fail to do so because you have been too busy coping
    with incoming paperwork?

3. In dealing with your backlog of paperwork, do you work through   Y / N
    the stack of papers on your desk from the TOP down picking
    out items which need attention?

4. When faced with uncomfortable paperwork, do you ever find   Y / N
    yourself dealing with lower pay-off, but more interesting items,
    first?

5. Does a piece of paper catching your attention out of the corner   Y / N
    of your eye often determine which item you deal with next?

6. When you are not at your desk, do items of unfinished   Y / N
    paperwork often spring into your conscious mind to remind you
    to deal with them the next time you are back in the office?

7. Have you given up using "to do" lists because they are more   Y / N
    trouble than they are worth?

8. Do you often stay late in the office or bring work home to try   Y / N
    and catch up on the backlog of paperwork?

9. Do you find that your job is too reactive for "to do" lists?   Y / N

10. If your working day was restricted to two hours, could you   Y / N
    produce a list — without hesitating — of the paperwork you
    would need to get done?

NOTE: Make a list of things "to do" EVERY DAY. Prioritize the activities on
      that list. Tackle the activities in order of decreasing pay-off.

Ask Yourself... "Does 80 percent of your results come from 20 percent of
your activities, or...?"

The Body Shop (in England) launched "PROJECT PAPERCHASE" to ensure that all reclaimable office waste paper was collected.

The project included:

1. Each desk (as far as practical) has two (2) bins (preferably of a different colour); one is "reclaimable" paper, the other is for all the "rubbish".

2. Each office zone has a project co-ordinator to check the consistent and proper segregation of reclaimable paper.

3. In each zone there is a central collecting bin into which every employee empties their reclaimable paper.

4. Cleaning staff transfer the reclaimable paper to a single storage area to await collection by a contractor.

Recycling your discarded paperwork is a socially, financially and rewarding exercise.

Steps to Take

(You might need to refer to page 48 for the five-folder method.)

1. Attack the paperwork mountain

2. Work through the "act on" stack

3. Work through the "pass on" stack

4. Work through the "file" stack

5. Deal with the "bin" stack

6. Eliminate multiple diaries

7. Deal with stationery items

8. Remove your in-tray from the desk

9. Shelve reference books / manuals

10. Designate your office a 'clutter-free' zone

Twelve Tips for Working More Effectively at Your Desk

- Write down your ideas. Do not trust your memory, no matter how good it may be!

- Set down your priorities before the start of each day's work.

- Use your high-productivity hours for your top-priority projects.

- Tackle time-consuming projects in stages.

- Do not over-schedule. Leave some time each day free from appointments.

- Concentrate on one item at a time.

- Take breaks. Walk around. Stretch. Eat lunch away from your desk.

- Establish a place for everything. Categorize, file, and store items nearby.

- Keep paperwork moving.

- Put limits on visits:

  - Stack stuff on any extra chairs so uninvited visitors have to stand.

  - When chatty people call, as soon as you answer the phone tell them you have only a few minutes to talk. Politely ask them the point of their call right away.

- Remove from your desk all papers you are not working on. This prevents lost or mixed-up papers.

- Handle each piece of paper only once.

Form Reduction Simplified

1. Publicize the form reduction process.

2. Set a target for the elimination of unnecessary forms.

3. Collect all forms.

4. Track each form through its life-cycle.

5. What is the purpose of each form?

6. Has means-end inversion occurred?

7. Evaluate form design.

8. Can the information be located elsewhere?

9. Form storage.

10.   Trial elimination.

Do the same with memos

Since emails are replacing memos, do treat emails as potential clutter, too.

Did You Know?
The Statistics on Filing Are Alarming

- People ignore up to 85 percent of the documents they retain.

- 45 percent of the documents we file are already filed elsewhere.

- Canadian businesses spend $500 million per annum to store over 170 million cubic metres of paper.

- In the US, there are over 300 billion documents on file with another 76 billion being added each year.

- A US study estimated that it costs $25,000 to print and process the forms in each four-drawer filing cabinet; $2,160 annually to maintain each cabinet.

Clear Your Filing Cabinet

Action plan

- Clear out all unnecessary paperwork from your filing system by DISCARDING it, passing it on, or by acting on it.

- Reorganize your files in order to locate papers quickly.

- Identify YOUR bad filing habits and take steps to eliminate them.

- Set time aside to clear/sort out your filing cabinet, papers, etc. Block out time in your diary/daytimer.

- Set a target for a major clear out for yourself and other staff members.

- Set up current action files.

Rate yourself on the following

Are you:

A discarder? _____

A hoarder? _____

Hopelessly disorganized? _____

Well organized? _____

What do you think OTHERS say about you regarding being organized?

_____

_____

How Effective Is Your Filing System?

Please tick in the box if you agree with each statement.

1. I often allow "to-file" paperwork to build up on my desk and only get around □
   to it when there is no more room on the desk.

2. I often have difficulty deciding what subject category to file under. □

3. I tend to leave paperwork on the desk rather than file it away. □

4. If I was absent from the office, my colleagues would have great difficulty □
   trying to locate information in my filing cabinet.

5. My filing system has grown in response to day-to-day requirements. I never □
   consciously planned a classification system to suit my needs.

6. My filing system contains documents which I rarely refer to and that could □
   quite easily be relocated elsewhere.

7. My filing system contains obsolete files. □

8. I have not cleared out my filing system in the past six months or more. □

9. I often file material for future reference but never use it again. □

10. On average, I spend more than 20 minutes a day trying to locate □
    documents from my desktop and filing system.

11. I sometimes have to complete a report from memory because I have lost a □
    draft or notes.

12. I have been known to file current action paperwork away and then forgot □
    about it.

13. I often go into meetings unprepared because I have not been able to locate □
    the background paperwork.

14. I have a huge stack of reading material building up around me in the office. □

15. When a project has been successful, I do not purge the project file. □

16. The labels in my filing system frequently cause confusion. □

17. There are a large number of folders in my filing cabinet that are bulging with □
    excess paperwork.

18. I have knowingly filed documents in the wrong folder because it was too □
    much trouble to find the correct one.

19. I have one drawer in my filing cabinet which is used as a "dump" drawer. □

20. I frequently lose pieces of paper that should have been filed. □

Do you use the principle "When in doubt, throw it out?"

How Much Time Do You Spend in a Typical Week?

	AVERAGE WORKING OFFICE		YOUR ESTIMATE	
	HRS	**MIN**	**HRS**	**MIN**
Writing	6	15	_____	_____
Reading	2	55	_____	_____
Calculating	2	35	_____	_____
Searching**	2	15	_____	_____
Mailing/Handling	2	45	_____	_____
Scheduling	1	40	_____	_____
File Retrieving	1	25	_____	_____
Delegating	1		_____	_____
Proofreading		55	_____	_____
Filing		50	_____	_____
	22	35	_____	_____

OTHER

    ** 24 minutes a day is spent looking for things on or around the desk!

Organize an in-company ...

Clear Your Desk Day

1. Set up a Clear Your Desk Day committee

2. Appoint Clear Your Desk co-ordinators

3. Make contacts with the paper merchants (recycle)

4. Adopt a Clear Your Desk policy

5. Decide on the date for your in-company Clear Your Desk Day

6. Organize Clear Your Desk workshops – 'Lunch & Learn' would be great!

7. Bring in an outside speaker/trainer (consider Paul Talbot)

8. Publicize the Clear Your Desk Day

9. Start to purge on bureaucratic paperwork

Good luck & have fun!

Coping with the Paperholic Boss

1. If you can, try to reduce the amount of paper that lands on the desk of your boss.

2. Keep an eye on the unfinished paperwork on the desk of your boss.

3. Use tactfully chosen signs.

4. Encourage your boss to plan more considerately.

5. Point out to your boss the negative effects of the clutter as they occur.

6. Reach an agreement with your boss on the different priorities of paperwork.

7. Ensure that you regularly review your priorities with your boss.

8. Get your boss to clear his/her desk.

9. Better still, send your boss to our seminar.

CLUTTER ACTION PLAN: REVIEW AND SELF-EVALUATION

Name: _____

Week of: _____ / _____

From   To

☐ **Household**   ☐ **Career**   ☐ **Health**
☐ **Lifestyle**   ☐ **Finances**   ☐ **Relationships**

1. **AREAS I WORKED ON THIS WEEK:** List the SUCCESSES that you have had this week. A success might be a project that you started or completed.

_____

_____

_____

_____

Did you remember to REWARD yourself at the end of each job/project completed?
Suggestion: Set a timeline for each item.

2. **AREAS I WILL WORK ON THIS COMING WEEK:** List projects that you wish to start or completed in the coming week. They are:

_____

_____

_____

_____

3. Remember to complete your CLUTTER ACTION PLAN each week.
4. Do not do zig-zag de-cluttering. Complete ONE task at a time BEFORE moving to the next one.
5. Give yourself a pat on the back, take a break and remember to REWARD YOURSELF (something consumable, dinner, a bottle of wine, breakfast, or a movie, massage or something "FUN")
6. A final word: Remember, Rome was not built in a day and your clutter will not disappear overnight. Be good to yourself, pace yourself and have patience.

GOOD LUCK!

Talbot's Tips

- When you take your clothes out of the dryer, fold them IMMEDIATELY.

- Make the inside of your closet pleasant. Use sachets where you store clothes.

CLEAR THE CLUTTER AND SIMPLIFY YOUR LIFE FOR SENIORS

INTRODUCTION

This workshop was born due to the increasing attendance of seniors and those nearing retirement. We discovered their needs differed greatly from those attending the basic "Clear the Clutter and Simplify Your Life©" which covered seven areas of clutter including job and career highlights which is often not a factor for this group of participants.

Many people attending this half-day workshop will fall into one or more of the following categories.

- Planning to downsize.

- Moving from the family home to an apartment.

- Moving into a retirement home.

- Moving in with a family member.

- Planning to live four to six months in Canada and spending the remainder of the time south, sometimes called snowbirds.

Moving, for any of us at any age can be difficult. This is especially true if we are moving from the family home filled with happy memories, to something that perhaps where we are alone.

So, before you start sorting, clearing, dumping and giving away stuff, you need to come up with a plan of action.

Where are you moving to? How much space do you have in storage? What are you going to take with you? Does it have value and purpose?

VALUE – This can be sentimental value. Hopefully the memories will he happy ones.

PURPOSE – Will you use it? If not, consider giving it to a family member or friend. Remember the stuff that you have might not be to the liking of your family or even your friends. Remember this so that you won't be offended if they tell you that they don't want it.

My suggestion:

You may have stuff from your parents or grandparents you might not have liked, but held on to it. Perhaps it is now worth something in cash value. Consider selling it and always try to obtain two prices so that you have something to compare. Use the Yellow Pages for antique dealers and secondhand dealers. Set a time for them to visit you, have a friend or family member with you and ask for the estimate in writing. They may give you a bulk or package price. Consider this option as well as a price for each individual item.

Many people that have done this have used the money for travelling, or have purchased something that they had always wanted. What will you do with your windfall?

If you give things to family and friends and you give it because you don't have the room for it in your new place, tell them you gave it so that they can become 'keepers' of the stuff. They can use the items and enjoy them, but you want to have visiting rights to it and perhaps you may want to personally use again.

If they are truly family and friends, they will have no problem accepting this.

To save people from fighting over your stuff at a later date, make a written list with a photograph (if possible) detailing the items that you intend to leave in your Will.

Clearing and sorting your clutter is a wonderful opportunity for you to update your Will. As you go through your stuff, make a note or name of the people you wish to give it to. Better yet, give it to them now. Why wait until you are gone unless you get tremendous pleasure from it and want to enjoy it while you can.

Special note

I have actually seen people go through drawers looking and fighting for stuff right after a memorial service. Don't let this happen to your family.

GETTING ORGANIZED

You will need:

- Empty boxes
- Garbage bags
- Markers and pens
- Labels

If possible, try and get a friend to help out, even if it is only to help sort things out.

Some of the boxes you can mark with labels such as:

- The name of the charity that you will be donating the items to.

- Friends and family members that you want to give the items to.

- Consignment stores – items that you want to try and get cash for. This can include clothing not worn such as outerwear and stuff you have held on.

Always ask yourself the question... Does this item have value or purpose for me?

CLOTHING

Going through your closets can be a nightmare. Stuff that you have not worn in years suddenly comes to life.

Rule of thumb...

If you have not worn clothing in the last twelve months, you can let it go. Be ruthless and make the decision to stick to it.

As you go through your clothing, look at your lifestyle. Perhaps you now wear clothing that is more casual, so the business suits with jackets you once wore, you no longer need. Ask yourself, "When was the last time I got all dressed up for a night out?" when you are considering evening wear. If this is still part of your lifestyle, then keep those items.

You can break your clothing into several categories such as:

- Daywear, both dressy and casual
- Elegant and dressy wear
- Evening wear

If you have no idea what to do, consider hiring an image consultant. If you are only thinking of losing weight, get rid of the items that do not fit.

At the same time, go through your outwear such as topcoats, both casual and dressy.

Do your shoes need fixing? Are the heels running down? Are they too tight, or need a good polishing? Ask a question and come up with a truthful answer.

How many bags do you have? More importantly, how many of them do you use?

As you continue to go through your stuff, make decisions and ask questions. Do you know, within your circle of friends and family, someone who would like this coat, bag or jacket? Decide and ask them. If they say no, you can give it to someone else or donate it to a charity of your choice.

Other considerations can include giving it to a charity where someone else will get value and purpose from it.

Jewellery

Perhaps you have some lovely jewellery and you would like your daughter, son, brother or sister to have. Can you let it go out of your life now? If not, them you will have to include this in your Will.

Often we find jewellery we own, but not worn for years. Perhaps your grandchild would like it. Again, you can make the choice and arrive at your own decision. Do it now!

Unused Gifts

In my experience, many seniors have gifts that are still wrapped or boxed, never used including underwear that they have purchased. Again, here is an opportunity to recycle your stuff either as a gift or just to give to a friend that you know who would not only use it, but also appreciate it.

Dinnerware and Silverware

Many seniors have wonderful dinnerware, silver or gold edged, but it can only be hand washed. In the fast pace that we live today, many people only use dinnerware that can be placed in the dishwasher. So, the elegant classy dinnerware that you own may not suit their lifestyle.

My suggestion:

As you go through your china cabinets, take the time to also go through your cupboards and take what you want. If you give dinner parties only once a year, perhaps you can let go of some stuff and either rent or borrow the rest when you need it.

Of course, as you start to go through your stuff, memories, both good, bad and indifferent will come back. Make a decision as to what you will keep and what must go. It is a hard decision to make, but it must be made.

First, ask your siblings if they would like any of the items. If the answer is "No", then ask the extended family, then the close friend(s). If they say "No", then try selling them.

Many China consignment stores will purchase well-named dinnerware. It is worth phoning around to check out these stores. One lady that took my course sold her dinnerware and was able to finance a trip to Europe. You might be pleasantly surprised what grandma's china is worth.

Now is the time to simplify your life. Take only what you need and what gives you pleasure in your life. Does it have value or purpose? Do you collect books, photos, plates or spoons? All of these items can have wonderful memories, but perhaps only to you.

BOOKS

This is very personal. You may wish to sort out the books from hard to soft back and then break them down into categories such as gardening, interior design, murder mysteries or autobiographies.

Ask yourself these questions when sorting:

- When was the last time I read this book?

- Will I re-read it again?

- Did I ever read this book?

- Will I ever need this book again?

- Who would love this book? Write down their name: I will donate this book to ... and name the charity, church, hospice, family or friend's name.

Perhaps now you are retired and have a very busy lifestyle; you may have taken up golf or other activities. Reading may be a lower priority on your list, so this may be a great opportunity to get rid of your books. Do it now!

COLLECT SPOONS, PLATES OR TEDDY BEARS?

You have collected these items for nearly all of your life. Now you are moving to a much smaller space that will not accommodate them. What do you do?

Ask yourself the question, "If my place burnt down to the ground and went up in smoke, how would I feel?" You would mostly likely miss them, but do they truly have value and purpose in your life?

Perhaps your son, daughter, bother, sister or good friend always admired them and often referred to them. Do you think that they would like them? Your concern is whether they would take good care of them as you have done. Could you part with them? Could you?

What are the alternatives if nobody wants them?

Consider selling them and turning the money into your dream travel fund. Perhaps donating them to an organization or library would not only reassure you that they were taken care of, but also give an opportunity to share them with other people.

FURNITURE

If you are considering moving or downsizing, much of your furniture may be too big and bulky for your new home. It is possible that you have owned the furniture for over twenty years and although you love it, it is time to let some of it go.

Think carefully about what items have either value or purpose. Would you use it? Consider family members or friends that have indicated their love for certain pieces of your furniture. Give it to them for at least you know that the items would be going to a good home and you could visit whenever you wanted to.

Often selling your furniture will not generate lots of cash. Nowadays, people do not want to pay a lot for second hand stuff. Again, using the Yellow Pages for dealers will give you an idea of what you can get for the items. Something is always better than nothing.

Moving and then using the second bedroom as a storage room is not the way to clear your clutter. Be realistic and take only what you need and share the other things with those that you love. The rest of the stuff is better off if you sell it.

PHOTOGRAPHS

These will have wonderful memories for you, but regrettably, many people do not identify photos with who, where or the date. This exercise takes a great deal of patience.

Photos are often left in drawers or filled to the brim in boxes. In order to sort photos out you must go through them one by one. At that time, you may wish to put them into a photo album marking them with the appropriate information. Duplicates of specific photos you may wish to hand over to a certain person. Photos make fine gifts and you may want to take the time to put something special together. Photographs hold so many memories and they may mean something different to each of us.

Treasure them, share them and above all, do something with them.

PERSONAL PAPERS

Imagine this ... if you died suddenly tomorrow (of course I hope you won't!) are your affairs in good order?

Do you have a Will?

Could your family find things?

Where do you keep paid and unpaid bills?

I worked with one lady that kept all her paid bills and receipts neatly filed by year, for the previous tens years, in zip lock bags. I asked her what was the value and purpose in keeping them. Her reply was that she didn't know, but it was how they were kept and it was how she was brought up.

Unless you need receipts and bills for tax purposes or for proof of warranty, throw the older ones away and use a shredder for disposing of them.

Clearing your clutter at this time is a wonderful opportunity to bring some order into your life and make it easier for others.

I know that some seniors do not want to confide their personal details with the family. Having a Will detailing who gets what and putting this into motion while you are alive will be of great value to everyone. At the same time this also can give you piece of mind.

FINANCES

Are your finances in good order? Could the family follow the paper trail? Do you have a safety deposit box and what do you keep in it? Is your bank passbook up to date? Is the bank's information about you accurate? Where is the copy of your Will? Have you made funeral arrangements and where is the information kept?

"Clearing the Clutter©" is all part of getting your house and affairs in order. It enables you to have total control over your personal effects and finances. It puts you in the driver's seat and determines who gets what.

For some people, they don't really care. I believe that by letting go and making a choice we are able to move ahead in our lives. More importantly, we are able to live it to the fullest without stuff and things getting in our way. Enjoy!

CHECK LIST 1: FURNITURE

Furniture items to give away or sell.

ITEMS (LIST)	TO WHOM (NAME)	DATE

CHECK LIST 2: HOUSEHOLD ITEMS

Household items to give away or sell. This includes pictures, carpets, rugs, mirrors, kitchen items and knick-knacks.

ITEMS (LIST)	TO WHOM (NAME)	DATE

CHECK LIST 3: DINNER-, CHINA-, SILVER-WARE

Dinnerware, chinaware and silverware. Best and everyday items to give away or sell.

ITEMS (LIST)	TO WHOM (NAME)	DATE

CHECK LIST 4: CLOTHING

Clothing items to give away or sell. This includes topcoats, shoes and bags.

ITEMS (LIST)	TO WHOM (NAME)	DATE

CHECK LIST 5: JEWELLERY

Jewellery items to give away or sell.

ITEMS (LIST)	TO WHOM (NAME)	DATE

CHECK LIST 6: IMPORTANT PAPERS

Items to be taken care of including: Will, power of attorney, funeral arrangements, bank accounts, name of bank or credit union all or any special instructions.

ITEMS (LIST)	ACTION TAKEN & OTHER DETAILS

CHECK LIST 7: OTHER ITEMS

Other items to give away or sell.

ITEMS (LIST)	TO WHOM (NAME)	DATE

Talbot's Tips

- Try doubling the recipe each time
  you make a dish.
  Freeze half, and pretty soon you will
  have enough in the freezer to take a
  week off!

- Have a basic tool kit available to do quick
  repair jobs like tightening screws and fittings,
  caulking, and hammering in nails that have
  loosened.

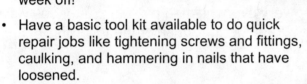

A FINAL WORD

The following is taken from an interview with Paul Talbot in *Shared Vision* for the 1998 issue.

> "Clutter can hold us back or help us grow because when we let go, our mind is clearer, thinking is clearer and we become more realistic and logical. We can take a look at our world the way it really is, rather than how we want it to be as we're holding onto the past. For some people, the way life is in the present is very difficult so they surround themselves with different forms of clutter like a buffer against the real world."

> "Do you feel guilty if you have clutter? Just realize that you are a unique individual. If it does bother you and you can't seem to deal with it, get someone else to do it for you."

If you are feeling very overwhelmed by your clutter you will need support and encouragement. Consider the following:

- Join a support group in your area.

- Consult our suggested reading list.

- Watch TV shows which focus on your areas.

- Re-read the chapters that are specifically applicable to you.

- Email the author with your issues. Your feedback might be included in the next edition of this book.

In the meantime, have fun!

SUGGESTED READING LIST

Getting Organized Books

Organizing for the Creative Person . . . . Dorothy Lehmkuhl and D. Cotter-Lamping

Getting Organized . . . . Stephanie Winston

Getting Your Act Together . . . . Pam Young and Peggy Jones

Best Organizing Tips . . . . Stephanie Winston

Taming the Paper Tiger (Organizing Paper in Your Life) . . . . Barbara Hemphill

Organizing Your Life . . . . Georgene Lockwood

Money and Financing Books

Money and the Meaning of Life . . . . Jacob Needleman

The Abundance Book . . . . John Randloph Price

Your Money or Your Life . . . . Joe Dominguez and Vicki Robin

Rich Dad, Poor Dad . . . . Robert Kiyosaki

The Wealthy Barber . . . . David Chilton

The Nine Steps to Financial Freedom . . . . Suzie Orman

Courage to Be Rich . . . . Suzie Orman

Work and Career

The Artist's Way at Work . . . . Mark Bryan and Julia Cameron

Building Your Field of Dreams . . . . Mary Manin Morrisey

Live the Life You Love . . . . Barbara Sher

To Build the Life You Want, Create the Work You Love . . . . Marsh Sinetar

What Colour Is Your Parachute . . . . Richard Nelson Bolles

Work with Passion . . . . Nancy Anderson

Books to Help You Move Forward with Your Life

Simple Abundance . . . . Sarah Ban Breathnach

True Love . . . . Robert Fulghum

Notes from a Friend . . . . Anthony Robbins

The Practice of Kindness . . . . Conari Press

Chicken Soup for the Soul . . . . Jack Canfield and Mark Victor Hanson

Dare to Be Yourself . . . . Alan Cohen

Simplicity Books

Health

Remember to... take time... for reflection... for beginnings... for nurturing... for discovery...

Because you are special!

"MABLE, I DON'T THINK THE "UNCLUTTER YOUR LIVES" PEOPLE MEANT FOR YOU TO GO THIS FAR!"

CONTACT INFORMATION

Paul Talbot is an international speaker / trainer and facilitator, published author, clutter therapist and simplicity coach.

To access his other resources now available, please log on to his website for full details, as well as Letters of References and Testimonials.

If you are seeking a speaker with an inspirational message and purpose for your next Lunch & Learn, Conference, Keynote or After-Dinner-Talk, remember ... Paul Talbot, A Speaker with a Purpose".

Contact Information in Canada:

Paul Talbot

PO Box 404

1195 Davie Street

Vancouver, BC, Canada

V6E 1N2

Email: admin@dialaspeaker.com

Website: www.dialaspeaker.com

CLUTTER

by Paul Talbot

I feel that life is rushing by,
as my clutter is getting high.

Why is this situation out of control,
because I know it's not good for the soul?

The books, boxes, clothing and papers too,
are some of the things I keep for you.

They're out of date and far too tight,
but I convince myself that it's alright.

Why am I holding onto this stuff,
it is because I felt life was rough?

I've had the stuff for many years,
to part with them would bring me to tears

My family and friends don't want my things,
only perhaps a few special rings.

I know I need to de-clutter my life,

and I would, if I could, just simplify!

There are lots of books on this subject for you,
but I need a course that offers support too.

"Clear the Clutter and Simplify Your Life"
was the course I took to change my life.

So as I start to de-clutter each day,
I feel the weight just lifting away.

Begin to enjoy the things we hold,
and share with loved ones as our new life unfolds.

The question we ask as we go through our stuff,
does it have value and purpose, and, can you be ruthless?

Each day is a gift, use it everyday,
share it with others and have your say.

So get rid of your clutter, don't save it, why?
You're a first class person so do it, and try.

Now is the time to say goodbye,
move on with your life and SIMPLIFY!

ISBN 142511220-X